THE
PROMISES
GAME

How to actually do
what you want to do!

Promise. Mean it.
Do it.

Valfrid Anderson &
Christopher Cudé

For Toby and Tiffany Ann, my two beagles, who were by my side most of the time I wrote this book. My best friends and companions -whom I miss very much. *Valfrid Anderson*

For my loving grandparents, Edward and Mary Helen Lynn. *Christopher Cudé*

ACKNOWLEDGEMENTS

So many people helped us develop and refine The Promises Game and write and edit this book. We are grateful for all of them. We would like to thank Judy Rowles, Cecelia Fusich, Kevin "Doogie" Cooper, Dorene Giacopini, Kevin and Stacey Cochrane, Stuart Anderson, Micha Stone, Garrett McCullough, Amanda and David Oroz, Christina Dougherty, Liam Springer Dougherty, Nate Grundman, D. Preston Wilson, Lien Chi Tran, Steven Gaglione, Jason Rodriguez, Susan Bernard, Donna Garr, Susie Franz, John Doebler, Jovanny Reyes, and Betsy Zimerman.

We also wish to thank everyone who has already played The Promises Game. Your efforts and successes have inspired and motivated us to write this book.

We also want to thank Randy Glasbergen for kindly allowing us to use his fantastic cartoons throughout the book. They made a big difference!

But finally, most of all, we want to thank Tina "Kitty" Courtney, one of the two people who played the very first Promises Game. Her enthusiasm, determination and success were critical to the creation of The Promises Game.

TABLE OF CONTENTS

INTRODUCTION

THE STORY BEHIND
THE PROMISES GAME

In 2003, I was bored. Things were going well in my life; in fact most things seemed great. My business was booming, I had just finished remodeling my house and I had shed 15 pounds. But I was still bored. Despite my successes, I wasn't *actually* doing what I wanted to do. So when I was invited to a seminar about transforming my life, I decided why not? It was great. I discovered a lot about myself. I also learned about the importance of integrity and keeping my word in order to actually do what I wanted to do in my life.

I was excited, but I'd been to many motivational seminars and few had permanently changed my life. This time was going to be different. But how? At the seminar, I met Kitty, and she felt the same way. We wanted to take that warm glow that we were feeling and turn it into something more than just a good memory. We were determined to take the principles we had learned and create some positive results in our lives. To actually do what we wanted to do.

One of the key things that we had learned at the seminar was about keeping your word, otherwise called keeping your Promises. If you say you're going to do something, make sure that you mean what you say and then *do it*.

We knew this was going to take some work. Over the next year and a half we worked through many different ideas and strategies to develop a plan or tool to help us actually do what we wanted to do by keeping Promises. Some of these ideas we had read or learned elsewhere and some we developed on our own. The final result was The Promises Game.

The Promises Game is a two-person, non-competitive game designed to help each player actually accomplish his or her goals and desires. There are no opponents. The other player is your partner, your *Promises Partner*. You will win or lose the game together. The rules are simple:

1. You will meet weekly with your Promises Partner and each of you will make a set of Promises that you are going to keep. You will start with three Promises each. Each person's Promises will be different. These Promises might be big or small, but they should be important to you.

2. One week later you will meet back together to share how you did that week keeping each of your Promises. If both of you kept each and every one of your Promises, you, as a team, move up to the next level (four Promises). If either one of you fails to keep even a single Promise, then, you as a team move down one level (two Promises).

3. You will continue week by week until you have completed the highest level - ten Promises for three consecutive weeks. That's how you win The Promises Game!

PROMISE. MEAN IT. DO IT.

PROMISE

A Promise is powerful. A Promise is much more than a goal or a wish or an item on a to-do list. A goal is something that you would like to do; something that you will work towards. A wish is just a dream. An item on a to-do list is just something you plan to do; if it's convenient. A Promise, on the other hand, is something that you will make every effort possible to keep at the risk of disappointing someone else. Have you ever been disappointed if someone didn't finish their to-do list one day? On the other hand, have you ever been upset if someone broke a Promise they made to you? Kitty and I decided to use Promises as a central tool in improving our lives.

Are you the type of person who Promises to be somewhere at 6:00 and no one expects you until 7:00. Or are you the type of person who Promises to be somewhere at 6:00 and if you haven't arrived by 6:05, people worry that you had an accident?

MEAN IT

You can't just make a Promise, you have to mean it. You have to intend, want and be able to keep your Promise. In today's world, the word Promise is too often just a fancy way to say "I want to" or "I hope to." It's an oft-abused word. We routinely accept someone's Promise as merely an expression of their hopes and expectations. We openly acknowledge the fact that our politicians' Promises mean almost nothing. We think it's normal if someone Promises to be somewhere on time and arrives only a half hour late.

It is useless to hold a person to anything he says while he is in love, drunk or running for office.

—Shirley MacLaine

The ability to say what you mean and mean what you say doesn't have a down side. A person who "means it" will be respected, honored and followed. They will gain integrity, confidence and conviction. In the end it's a choice that you make each day. Do you just say it or do you mean it?

Kitty and I wanted to use the true meaning of Promise to make our lives better. The Promises that we would make would mean something. We intended to keep those Promises. We would be accountable to each other for those Promises.

DO IT

It's not enough to make a Promise. It's not enough to mean your Promise; you have to keep your Promise. You have to *do it*. The Promises Game uses accountability to help you keep your Promises. Being held accountable is effective. Nobody likes to let someone else down.

Accountability and Weight Loss

Josh has lost over one hundred twenty pounds recently. He joined Weight Watchers and exercised religiously. As part of the program, he would go in each week to be weighed by the Weight Watchers' staff. The weigh-ins were very low-key; they just weighed him and recorded the results. After several months he had lost a lot of weight. For the next two months, he continued the exact same diet and exercise plan, but no longer went in for his weekly weigh-ins. To Josh's surprise he didn't lose a single pound in those two months. He thought he was doing everything the same, but his results were different. The difference was accountability. Josh said that knowing that he was going to be weighed literally caused him not to put food in his mouth.

MAKE IT A GAME

The Promises Game has rules and winners, and successes and failures - but no losers. It's a non-competitive game without an opponent.

Everyone enjoys a game more than a dull exercise. So Kitty and I decided to make a game out of it. We only had each other, so our team was just the two of us. However, we weren't living together, we didn't work at the same place and our lives didn't intersect very much. It was impractical for us to work together on the same goals. So rather than work together on the same Promises, we decided to work separately on our own personal Promises and report back to each other on our results. By keeping all of our Promises, we could then move forward in the game.

I have found the use of turning activities into a game often works like magic. I tutor middle school kids and one of my students, who is very bright, just doesn't like reading, writing, and especially grammar and spelling. However, he does love baseball. To keep his interest, I came up with a grammar baseball game. I prepared various single, double, triple and homerun grammar and spelling questions. The questions were usually about things we had studied earlier or that he was having problems with. We made it a game and kept score. He's now getting A's on his English tests instead of D's. We made a game out of one of the dullest activities in a student's routine and it worked.

THE PROMISES GAME WORKS

After Kitty and I finished and won the first Promises Game, each of us moved on to play the game with someone else. Kitty's second partner was Christopher Cudé. Christopher and I are the co-authors of this book. From there many, many people have played The Promises Game and it has made a big difference in most of their lives. The game spread because others saw the results and wanted to create the same for themselves.

The Promises Game will work for you. People playing The Promises Game have found new and better jobs, remodeled and sold homes, lost weight, traveled far and wide, improved their tennis games, strengthened their relationships and made new friends. They have accomplished any number of other things; some great, some small, but always important to them. You will love playing The Promises Game. It's amazing how much you'll get done. You will actually do what you want to do.

In Chapter One we will explain what The Promises Game is and how you play the game.

PROMISE. MEAN IT. DO IT.

But I have promises to keep,

And miles to go before I sleep,

And miles to go before I sleep.

—Robert Frost

PART ONE

THE BASICS

HOW TO USE THIS BOOK

This book is divided into three parts. Part One is about the basics of The Promises Game. Here you will find the rules and mechanics of the game as well as what makes for a good Promise. Once you have finished Part One, you will be ready to play the game. Use the Weekly Promises Logs in the Appendix to start playing.

Part Two is a selection of chapters that discuss sample or example Promises for many different areas of your life. Most people that start playing The Promises Game come up with their first several Promises fairly easily. After a few weeks, however, they are looking for some new ideas. Use Part Two to help you select Promises that others have made and get inspiration for your own Promises. It will give you some great suggestions for Promises that might not occur to you otherwise. You will not need to read Part Two until you have started playing the game yourself.

Part Three has some additional information and suggestions for playing. We look into the different forms of Promises. We also present several helpful hints and suggestions for playing the game. These chapters will be most valuable to you once you have played for a couple of weeks.

Finally there is an Appendix – Weekly Promises Logs. Use the Weekly Promises Logs to track your Promises and get started playing the game.

CHAPTER ONE

HOW TO PLAY
THE PROMISES GAME

It's New Year's Eve. John has had a glass or two of champagne. He's feeling pretty good about his life. But this New Year is the year that he's going to lose some weight, pay off his credit cards and travel to Europe. So how will he do this? Ah-ha! He knows the secret. He'll make three New Year's resolutions right at midnight. It's the sure-fire way to really do what he wants to do. Three hundred sixty-five days later, what are the odds that he will have kept his three New Year's resolutions?

The Promises Game is for anyone who has ever read a self-help book. This game will show you how to make those self-help books work for you and to finish what you start. This game is for people who are busy all day long, but aren't living the lives they really want to lead. It will help them focus on what matters. The Promises Game is for people like John who make New Year's resolutions. How great would it be to actually keep your New Year's resolutions?

> **Regularly keeping your Promises, otherwise called reliability or dependability, is a character trait. Like all character traits, it must be acquired and nurtured. No one has ever been born reliable.**

So how do you play The Promises Game? What are the rules? How will you know if and when you have won the game? That's what this chapter is all about - the rules and mechanics of playing The Promises Game. First we will discuss whom to pick to play the game with, as well as how to approach him or her. Then, we will discuss when you meet together and the actual rules of the game. Finally we will show you how you win The Promises Game. In Chapter Two we will discuss what makes for a good Promise.

SELECTING A PROMISES PARTNER

You first need to select a Promises Partner. This is the person that you will be playing The Promises Game with and selecting him or her is one of the most important steps in the game. Select someone who is serious about accomplishing things in his or her life, willing to make commitments and able to carry through.

Who could be your Promises Partner? It might be:

- Your best friend

- Your second best friend

- A co-worker

- Your neighbor

- Someone from your church

- A classmate

- Your brother, sister or cousin

- Someone on your softball team

- Someone from your AA meeting

- An acquaintance

Your Promises Partner doesn't need to be perfect. You do not need to know each other well. Your daily lives should not intersect in too many areas. You do not need to be completely separate, but constant contact is not ideal either. Your spouse or boss are not good choices.

How do you approach someone to ask them to be your Promises Partner?

1. Give them a brief overview of the game.

2. Have them read Part One (Chapters One and Two) of this book. You only need to read the first two chapters to get started. The remaining chapters will help you as you continue to play the game.

3. Set a date, time and place for your first Promises Meeting, preferably within a week.

The Promises Game is not for everyone and some people just aren't interested. If that is the case, then just move along to find someone else; it won't take long to find a good Promises Partner. The important thing is that you don't complicate the process. Waiting to find the 'perfect' Promises Partner is just an excuse to procrastinate! Find someone who wants to accomplish more in their life and start playing the game.

YOUR FIRST PROMISES MEETING

At your first Promises Meeting, each of you will verbally make three Promises to each other. Before your first Promises Meeting, you should sit down and decide what three Promises you intend to make for that week. Write them down. In the Appendix we have Weekly Promises Logs that you can use to get started and track your Promises. Make sure that your Promises are objective and quantifiable. Also make sure they are something that you know you can get done. Do not Promise something that you know you were already going to do that week. The purpose of a Promise is to create *additional, new* results in your life.

> *I think this is the beginning of a beautiful friendship.*
>
> **—Rick Blaine (Humphrey Bogart), Casablanca**

Formalizing your Promises in person is important because once you voice them, you have made a Promise. Your clarity of purpose is imperative to your success. Try not to hold a Promises Meeting over the phone or by email. When making a Promise it is important to be able to look your Promises Partner in the eye and state the Promise you intend to keep. Personal interaction is essential. Make your Promises Meetings in person as often as possible.

Post Your Promises.

Keep a list of your Promises or, preferably, your Weekly Promises Log, somewhere where you will see it often. Post it on the bathroom mirror, on your desk or on your refrigerator.

At the end of your first Promises Meeting you will set the time and place for your next meeting. Whenever possible it is a good idea to select the same day of the week and approximately the same time of day. Of course that is not always practical. It's all right to shorten the time to six days or extend it to eight or nine days, as necessary. The time of your next Promises Meeting is not itself a Promise. If something comes up during the week, it is acceptable to adjust the time or location. One pair of Promises Partners who lived about 30 minutes apart, decided to meet somewhere new and interesting in between their homes each week.

PROMISES KEPT - PROMISES BROKEN

At the end of the first week, you will meet again with your Promises Partner to share whether or not you kept all three of your Promises. You will probably not have had a lot of direct contact with your Promises Partner throughout the week. *It is not your Promises Partner's duty to help you keep your Promises. It is your responsibility to keep your Promises.* Your Promises Partner does not monitor your results throughout the week. You do not need to give each other progress reports.

If at the end of the first week both of you have kept *all* three of your Promises *"in excellence"* (more on this term later) - congratulations! Both of you, as a team, move up to the next level. For the next week each of you will make four Promises to each other. If either of you break even one Promise, then both of you move down to two Promises for the next week. If you fail to keep a Promise own it. Take responsibility for your failure and learn from it. For the next week you should be invigorated to make smarter choices and keep all of your Promises. Don't give up and learn from your mistakes.

Two Promises is the fewest Promises in any given week.

WINNING THE PROMISES GAME

Your results are scored as a team. Your final goal will be to keep *ten* Promises each for *three* consecutive weeks.

Here is a chart that represents a typical Promises Game progression.

WEEK 1	3 PROMISES
WEEK 2	All Promises Kept - 4 PROMISES
WEEK 3	All Promises Kept - 5 PROMISES
WEEK 4	Both partners did not keep all of their Promises - Back down to 4 PROMISES
WEEK 5	All Promises Kept - 5 PROMISES
WEEK 6	All Promises Kept - 6 PROMISES
WEEK 7	Skipped this week because one of the partners went on vacation
WEEK 8	7 PROMISES
WEEK 9	One partner did not keep all of his Promises - Back down to 6 PROMISES
WEEK 10	All Promises Kept - 7 PROMISES
WEEK 11	All Promises Kept - 8 PROMISES
WEEK 12	All Promises Kept - 9 PROMISES

WEEK 13	All Promises Kept - 10 PROMISES
WEEK 14	All Promises Kept - 10 PROMISES
WEEK 15	All Promises Kept - 10 PROMISES

CONGRATULATIONS!

YOU HAVE WON THE PROMISES GAME

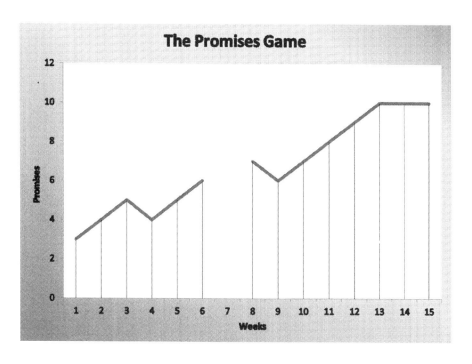

When you, as a team, have both kept ten Promises for three consecutive weeks, you and your Partner have won The Promises Game. Don't be scared of ten Promises. Often when people think of Promises, they envision things that take a lot of time - perhaps several hours each. If you plan to make Promises that will take four hours each in a week, ten Promises will be 40 hours - a full-time job. If you already have a job, that won't work. The majority, perhaps even all of your Promises should each not add more than ten minutes of extra effort to your life in a week. Some Promises could be time-intensive; but most should be quick. It's easy to spend no more than one hour of extra effort in a week to keep ten Promises. We will show you how throughout the rest of this book.

Rewards and Awards: The Promises Game is very rewarding in and of itself. You will be amazed how good it feels to keep each Promise. Some people also like to give each other a reward for winning the game. It should be something memorable and out of the ordinary. Maybe a dinner out at a nice restaurant together or a trip to a fun place. A plaque, a gift, a piece of art, or some award to celebrate your victory would work well too. Not everyone needs a reward or an award. The greatest reward for winning is *actually doing what you want to do.*

> *Just play. Have fun. Enjoy the game.*
>
> **—Michael Jordan**

THE PROMISES GAME.ORG

Our website is ThePromisesGame.org. We will be regularly providing further insights and suggestions, including videos, for playing The Promises Game. You will find new sample Promises and links to related websites that can help you play the game. Finally we will try to answer any questions you might have about the game. Please visit us at ThePromisesGame.org.

> *Far and away the best prize that life offers is the chance to work hard at work worth doing.*
>
> **—Theodore Roosevelt**

PROMISE. MEAN IT. DO IT.

CHAPTER TWO

WHAT'S A GOOD PROMISE?

GLASBERGEN   Copyright 2011 by Randy Glasbergen.

"My goal is to start exercising by the
1st of Someday and lose ten pounds
by the day after Eternity."

A good Promise should be objective and quantifiable. A good Promise should be selected carefully. Think about what you want to accomplish in the next week. A Promise is not a goal. A Promise is a Promise. The reason a Promise is not a goal is because a goal is something that you want to accomplish, something that you hope to do. A Promise is something that you Promise to do (or not to do, as the case may be). You Promise to do *whatever it takes* to keep your Promise. You work towards a goal; you keep a Promise. So choose your Promises wisely and mean it. Your first three Promises are three things that you *will* accomplish this week.

It's ok to repeat the same Promise over again. Sometimes, it's even necessary. See Chapter Five on habits.

Objective and Quantifiable: A Promise must be objective and quantifiable, not subjective. By this we mean you should be able to clearly determine whether or not you have kept your Promise. You can quantify "running five miles on the treadmill" with reasonable certainty. You cannot quantify "working out hard this week." Subjective goals are important in this world, but they do not fit well into the structure of The Promises Game. Stick to objective Promises that have quantifiable results. Choose "read my son three bedtime stories" not "spend more quality time with my son." Choose "go to the gym four times this week" not "concentrate on working out." Choose "clean the hall closet" not "stop being messy."

Sometimes you may want to accomplish something that really takes more than one week to finish. You can split a project in half, so long as each half can be fully completed within a week. For example, if your goal is to read a long book, your first week's Promise could be to read chapters one through five. After the first week is over, you could make a new Promise to read chapters six to the end. Splitting a Promise into two or more parts is a great way to accomplish larger projects.

Here are some examples of good Promises to start with:

- I PROMISE TO JOIN A GYM THIS WEEK.

- I PROMISE TO BALANCE MY CHECKBOOK.

- I PROMISE TO FLOSS MY TEETH EVERY DAY.

- I PROMISE TO MAKE MY BED EVERY MORNING BEFORE I GO TO WORK.

- I PROMISE TO COOK A ROMANTIC DINNER FOR MY GIRLFRIEND.

- I PROMISE TO GO TO CHURCH THIS SUNDAY.

- I PROMISE TO FLY A KITE IN THE PARK.

Be careful what you Promise: Before you make a Promise take some time to think about the consequences of that Promise. How much time will be involved? How big is this Promise? Is this really something that you want to accomplish? Are you pushing yourself hard enough? Are you pushing yourself too hard? Are there any potential conflicts that could interfere with your ability to keep this Promise?

A Clean Garage

John once Promised to thoroughly clean his garage. It hadn't been properly cleaned in years. What he expected to take an hour would take an entire day. Fortunately he had the full day available. A quick check of the garage *before* he made that Promise would have made it clear to him that he was making a much larger Promise than he anticipated. He

was surprised by the magnitude of his Promise. He
could have revised the Promise to make it more reasonable. But sometimes mistakes have their upsides.
He did get a really clean garage.

The majority of your Promises should each not add more than
ten minutes of extra effort to your life in a week. A couple of Promises could be time-intensive; but most should be quick (more on
what makes a Promise quick later in this chapter). Take a look
ahead at your time commitments before you make your Promises.

Exceptions: Are there any exceptions to the rule that you must
keep a Promise? As a general rule, no. Procrastination is definitely
not an exception. Get to work right away so that unexpected circumstances do not get in the way. Front-load your Promises (that
is start what you can as early as possible in the week) and plan your
Promises with potential conflicts in mind. In Chapter Twelve we
will give you a lot of helpful hints on how to keep your Promises
and how to make Promises that you will be able to keep.

Mystery Promises: You may also have Promises that you would
like to make, but want to keep personal. It is acceptable to select
a mystery Promise. Perhaps this Promise deals with confidential
information involving work or other people. In this case you would
simply make a mystery Promise without going into details. You
would monitor your compliance by yourself. At the next Promises
Meeting you would tell your Promises Partner whether or not you
kept the mystery Promise, but not share the details. You should use
mystery Promises sparingly and limit yourself to no more than one
per week.

In Excellence: A Promise must be kept *in excellence*. A Promise
envisions not only accomplishing something to be able to "check it
off the list," but also to finish it in such a way that you are proud
of the results. It also must fulfill the intent behind your decision to
make that Promise. *In excellence* is the subjective aspect of a Prom-

ise. A Promise is only kept if you have fully completed the Promise consistent with the spirit behind it. You cannot just go through the motions. It will be up to you to decide if you have completed a Promise *in excellence.*

The Bathroom Ceiling

One week Susan made a Promise to clean the upstairs bathroom. It was a busy week for her but she had been watching the mold build up on the ceiling above the shower. She realized that it probably wasn't going to move out on its own. Susan cleaned the bathroom, reorganized the drawers, scoured the tub and sprayed the mold with bleach. She felt good about her efforts but she could still see where the mold had once been and the ceiling was all spotted from the bleach. The next day she looked up at the ceiling and decided this was not *excellence.* She got the ladder and repainted the ceiling. When she finished the bathroom had never looked better. She smiles every time she looks at that ceiling. That extra effort created *excellence.*

Writing The Promises Game

"One week I Promised to finish writing a chapter in this book. Yes, I used The Promises Game to help write *The Promises Game.* It wasn't one of my most creative weeks to say the least and on top of that I procrastinated until the last day. I finished that chapter, but when I read what I had written, I crumpled up the paper. I had definitely failed the *excellence* test. Promise not kept." *Valfrid*

FORMAT OF PART TWO

Let's take a moment to introduce the format that we are going to be using for Part Two. We will introduce a general topic, in the first chapter (Chapter Three) it is weight loss and getting in shape. We will share a few of our thoughts and experiences. Then we will list at least 15 standard, run-of-the-mill Promises that relate to that general topic. These are actual Promises that someone has made and kept in the past.

Standard Promises

A standard Promise is a simple straightforward Promise that we have made or that one of our Promises Partners has made over the years. They are meant to give you some ideas about Promises related to that chapter's general topic. Feel free to adapt them to your specific circumstances. For example, one of our sample Promises is to do 100 sit-ups each day. For some people, that may be far too many sit-ups to do daily. For others, twice as many sit-ups might not be enough. There is no magic to 100 sit-ups. Make it your Promise with the correct number for you. After some of the sample Promises we will sometimes add comments to clarify that Promise or detail some of our experiences with that particular Promise.

After setting out 15 standard Promises, we will list at least five Promises that are either quick or even create time.

Quick Promises

A quick Promise is a Promise that essentially takes no significant amount of time. It might be a Promise to make a quick phone call to set up an appointment. No matter how busy you are, you should have time to make a one minute phone call. Or it might be a Promise *not* to do something. You can't complain that you don't have enough time not to eat candy bars. Remember, a majority, even most of your Promises should be quick Promises (or even time-creating Promises). Use these suggestions to find enough quick Promises to make in any given week.

Time-Creating Promises

A time-creating Promise is a Promise that not only doesn't really take up any time, but instead, adds more time to your day. For example, getting up a half-hour earlier each day gives you 30 extra minutes each day. You also can't complain that you don't have enough time in the day to wake up earlier.

Creative Promises

Creative Promises are Promises that are *outside the box.* With a creative Promise you want to use your imagination to expand the topic. Many of the creative Promises we will share are Promises that we have made ourselves and some are Promises that we hope to make in the future. It's ok and we encourage you to have some fun, so don't be afraid to think outside the box every now and then and throw in a creative

Promise to keep things interesting. So, finally in each chapter, we will list at least five *creative* Promises regarding that chapter's general topic.

> *Odd how the creative power at once brings the whole universe to order.*
>
> **—Virginia Woolf**

THAT'S ALL FOLKS!

That's all there is to The Promises Game. It is really very simple and straightforward, but it is one of the most powerful tools you will ever use. If you put this book down right now you could start playing The Promises Game and the game would start working for you. We will clarify a lot of the questions you may have in the next several chapters. There will be lists of sample Promises for you in many different areas of your life. You can pick any number of your Promises from these lists, or just come up with your own unique Promises. If your Promises Partner comes up with a great Promise, you could make that Promise yourself sometime.

So get ready to play The Promises Game. You will be amazed at what you will accomplish in a short period of time. All you need is to find your Promises Partner, decide on your first three Promises and you're ready to go.

PROMISE. MEAN IT. DO IT.

PART TWO

PROMISES, PROMISES
A REFERENCE GUIDE

Welcome to Part Two. By now you have been playing The Promises Game for a couple of weeks. When you started playing the game you had a handful of things that you wanted to do. Hopefully, you have finished or are on the way to finishing most of those desires. But now you need to make five or six Promises and you may have run out of fresh ideas. Now it is time to put Part Two to work for you.

Over the years we have made or witnessed hundreds of different Promises in wide and varied areas of people's lives. Sometimes our Promises Partner made such a great Promise that we chose to make the same Promise in the next week. We kept track of all of these Promises that anyone made. We share them with you in this Part Two to inspire you to make your own Promises.

We have divided these actual Promises into several different areas of your life. The first chapter is about weight loss and getting in shape; the next one is about your finances. Use these actual Promises to inspire and motivate you. Discover the possibilities you can achieve in your life playing The Promises Game. And have fun at the same time. If you need inspiration for one or more of your Promises this week choose a chapter that deals with an area of your life that you want to concentrate on. Feel free to adapt the Promises to your own unique circumstance. Or you can make the Promise exactly the way it was made by someone else in the past.

I thought of a bunch of things I need to do just by reading the various promise examples. I read them and realized I need to wash the car, or call my aunt, or something. They are great.

—Kevin C.

CHAPTER THREE

LET'S GET PHYSICAL AND LOSE SOME WEIGHT

"Eat less and exercise more? That's the most ridiculous fad diet I've heard of yet!"

Every New Year the airwaves are filled with ads for gyms, weight loss services and diet pills. Gyms have their highest attendance and the most new memberships in

> **According to the Center for Disease Control (CDC), in 2006, 33% of adult males and 35% of adult females in the U.S. were obese.**

January. It seems like everyone wants to lose weight or get into shape in the first couple of weeks of the year. By February, these ad campaigns are over and the gyms are back to regular attendance. The desire to lose weight or get into shape didn't go away, most people just found it easier *not to* go to the gym than to go.

Promises about weight loss and getting in shape are the most common Promises made by people playing The Promises Game. In fact, we can't recall a single game where one of the Promises Partners didn't make at least one Promise related to losing weight or getting in shape. Playing The Promises Game is great for weight loss and getting in shape because it will keep you in the gym through February and all the way into the summer.

Getting in shape may mean developing a healthy lifestyle to live longer and better. It could also be part of a specific physical goal such as running a marathon or excelling at a sport. Or maybe you want to get in shape because you want to look good. No matter what your reason for getting into shape, The Promises Game is the tool that will help you bridge the gap between wanting to get in shape and *actually* getting in shape.

You might want to lose weight because you're ten pounds overweight and don't ever want to be 50 pounds too heavy - you want to take preventative action. You may have to lose weight because you are 50 pounds overweight and your health is at risk. Or maybe you want to lose weight because you want to look good – vanity has its place.

> **If you never gain ten extra pounds, it's impossible to gain 50 extra pounds.**

DIET AND EXERCISE

To lose weight or get into shape you will need to decide upon a diet and exercise plan. Ultimately, to lose weight, you have to find a way to expend more calories than you consume. Getting in shape might involve losing some weight or maybe just eating better food. In both cases, an exercise plan is equally important. Use your weekly Promises to implement this diet and exercise plan. Week by week you will get closer to you desired results.

> **The Promises Game Diet – Eat Less and Exercise More.**

We have had a lot of success with *The South Beach Diet*, developed by Dr. Agatston. We both have consistently used *The South Beach Diet*, in conjunction with The Promises Game and have been very pleased with our results. There are a lot of great diets out there (and bad ones as well). Choose the diet that works best for you and use The Promises Game to stick to that diet.

> **The CDC recommends two and a half hours moderate aerobic exercise and two days of muscle-strengthening activity every week.**

Exercise might include working out with weights, jogging, yoga or any number of activities. We have used The Promises Game to consistently go to the gym, attend spinning classes and run miles on the beach. It's a lot easier to go to the gym or jog every other day when you make it a Promise (especially when it's cold and rainy outside).

How can you determine if you are overweight? You could check your body/mass index. Go to *cdc.gov/healthyweight*

COLD AND RAINY DAYS

Little of what we have been discussing in the chapter so far should be new to you. You probably already know how to lose weight or get into shape. How is that working for you? It's one thing to know what you want to achieve – it's quite another thing to *actually* do it. That's where The Promises Game comes into play.

If you want to lose twenty pounds, you can't just go to the gym one afternoon and lose all twenty pounds. It will take a plan, determination and time. You might even need the help of professionals, such as a personal trainer or a weight lose service, to achieve your results. Whatever route you choose, you can break it down into weekly Promises. If your plan is solid you will eventually reach your desired result by keeping your Promises one day at a time and one week at a time. The Promises Game is especially helpful on cold and rainy days when you are looking for an excuse to stay home.

Back to his College Weight

At 6'2" and 205 pounds, Brad was about fifteen pounds heavier than he wanted. So he developed an aggressive workout plan at the gym and started on *The South Beach Diet.* He made weekly Promises to his Promises Partner regarding one or more aspects of his weight loss program. One week he Promised to go to the gym four times. Another week he Promised not to eat certain foods that were restricted on his diet. Slowly but surely, he met his goal of 190 pounds. Later he started up another program and got down to his college weight of 178. He'd been trying for years to lose that extra weight, but it took The Promises Game to actually lose it.

Running a Half Marathon

Jessica was in pretty good shape, but she was ready to take it to the next level. There was a half marathon coming up in a couple of months and she wanted to participate. She first made a Promise to find a new gym. She decided to join a *CrossFit* gym and started going regularly. She met with a trainer and made weekly Promises to implement the diet and workout plan her trainer had given her. She not only completed the half marathon but she continued to use The Promises Game to stay in shape. Her next goal is a full marathon.

If you want to lose weight or get into shape and if you have trouble coming up with Promises in any given week, look over these sample Promises and select one that works for you. Modify one to fit your circumstances or feel free to make it in exactly the form we present here.

Here are 15 sample standard Promises regarding weight loss and getting in shape.

FIFTEEN STANDARD PROMISES

- I PROMISE TO JOIN A GYM THIS WEEK.

    This is simple. You will be able to determine definitively whether you joined the gym.

- I PROMISE TO GET UP BY 6:00 A.M. THREE TIMES THIS WEEK AND WORK OUT.

    This is a compound Promise. You must keep both parts (getting up by 6:00 a.m. and working out) to keep this Promise. Make sure that both components of a compound Promise are important to you. Compound Promises are further explained in Chapter Eleven.

- I PROMISE TO SPEND A TOTAL OF TWO HOURS THIS WEEK DOING CARDIO EXERCISES AT THE GYM.

    This is an aggregate Promise. By this we mean that you intend to spend, in total, two hours doing cardio exercises. You probably don't intend to do the full two hours at once. You might keep this Promise by working out for 30 minutes one day, 20 minutes another two days, and 25 minutes for two more days for an aggregate of 120 minutes that week. Aggregate Promises are further explained in Chapter Eleven.

- I PROMISE TO DO 100 SIT-UPS EACH DAY.

    Obviously the number you chose is up to you. You are not limited to sit-ups. Push-ups or pull-ups or even back flips all work.

- I PROMISE TO TAKE A ONE HOUR BIKE RIDE IN THE COUNTRY.

- I PROMISE TO CREATE A NEW WORKOUT PLAN AND DO IT TWICE.

> Creating detailed and well-thought-out plans for doing something is a great type of Promise. We definitely encourage it. However, don't just plan to do something, try to do something concrete to implement your plan. In this case, you are Promising to actually create a workout plan *and* perform it twice. If you can't actually start your plan, at least Promise to write it down.

- I PROMISE TO SWIM 40 LAPS IN THE POOL.

- I PROMISE TO WALK TO WORK THREE DAYS THIS WEEK.

> If that's not feasible maybe bicycling to work would be an alternative. If work is still too far away, maybe walk or bike to the gym or some other place that you go to regularly that is within walking or riding distance.

- I PROMISE TO ATTEND MY FIRST YOGA CLASS.

- I PROMISE TO GET RID OF ALL THE JUNK FOOD IN MY KITCHEN.

> You decide what you consider to be junk food. You may want to make this Promise a little more specific to clarify exactly what it is that you want to eliminate. And by the way, we think that *eating* the junk food would violate the spirit of "getting rid" of all the junk food.

- I PROMISE NOT TO EAT ANY FAST FOOD.

> Twelve hundred calorie supersized meals don't belong in anyone's diet if they are trying to lose weight.

- I PROMISE TO EAT ONLY WHOLE WHEAT BREAD, NOT WHITE BREAD.

- I PROMISE NOT TO EAT AFTER 9:00 P.M.

   How often have we heard that eating late at night is a bad idea if you want to lose weight. We aren't sure if it's true, but it sure seems to be accurate at least in our experience. Google "eat late at night" for a wealth of information on why it's a bad idea to eat too much before going to bed.

- I PROMISE TO EAT BREAKFAST EVERY DAY.

   The same as eating late at night can be a bad way to lose weight, starting each day with a good breakfast can actually help you lose weight. Two cups of coffee probably doesn't count as eating breakfast.

- I PROMISE TO BUY AND USE THREE *LEAN* OR *DIET* ENTREES FROM THE GROCERY STORE.

   Boy we have come a long way from those TV dinners from the seventies that resembled cardboard more than food! Today these meals actually taste good and can be healthy for you as well. These are meant to be meals though, not appetizers.

FIVE QUICK OR TIME-CREATING PROMISES

- I PROMISE NOT TO EAT ANY DOUGHNUTS.

- Substituting ice cream for doughnuts doesn't count. I PROMISE TO COOK WITH OLIVE OIL INSTEAD OF BUTTER.

- I PROMISE NOT TO STOP OR WALK DURING MY JOGS.

- I PROMISE TO DO 200 ISOMETRIC EXERCISES AT MY DESK EACH DAY.

  > Isometric exercises are static muscle contractions that exercise the muscles usually without using weights. Squeezing your stomach repeatedly to build abdominal muscle tone is an example of an isometric exercise.

- I PROMISE TO WEIGH MYSELF EACH MORNING AND WRITE IT DOWN.

  > You weigh yourself daily, not to see how many pounds you lost in the previous 24 hours but to see the pattern over time. Any one day can be an aberration. But over time, the pattern will be clear. That's why it's important to write it down. You can see the readings that are outside the pattern and you ignore them. Also be consistent in your weighing habits. The best time is first thing in the morning before you eat or drink anything and after you go to the bathroom. Two full glasses of water that you drink in the morning (or two full glasses of beer from the previous night that are still in you) could weigh almost two pounds. Always use the same scale.

FIVE CREATIVE PROMISES

- I PROMISE TO TAKE TWO *BEFORE* PICTURES OF MYSELF IN A SWIMSUIT.

  > Don't underestimate the motivating power of a *before* picture. It also provides the later reward when you

can pair it with a successful *after* picture in the same swimsuit.

- I PROMISE TO GO OUT DANCING ONE NIGHT AND DANCE NON-STOP FOR A SOLID HOUR.

- I PROMISE TO KEEP A LOG OF WHAT I EAT AND DRINK THIS WEEK.

  We are often surprised how simply writing something down can change your behavior. If you have to write down each soda you drink or candy bar you eat, you will probably drink less soda and eat less candy. Even if you don't, you have the information you need for the next week's Promise for eliminating or reducing certain items from your diet. The log can be as detailed or as general as you want to make it. You can keep it to yourself or decide to share it with someone else. That someone else could be your Promises Partner or your roommate. Whatever works for you. There are even apps to keep these logs. Check out *MyFitnessPal, Lose It!* or *Tap & Track.*

- I PROMISE TO CREATE A MOTIVATIONAL PLAYLIST FOR MY IPOD TO PLAY DURING MY WORKOUTS.

- I PROMISE TO DETERMINE FIVE FOODS THAT I EAT REGULARLY THAT HAVE TOO MANY CALORIES OR TOO MUCH FAT AND FIND SUITABLE LOWER CAL-ORIE OR LOWER FAT SUBSTITUTES AND I PROM-ISE TO TRY ALL FIVE SUBSTITUTES THIS WEEK.

  These are all sample Promises that you could make in any given week regarding weight loss and getting in shape. Most of these Promises are ones that we ourselves have made or that someone else has made at one time or another. The idea here is to spur your imagination and start your creative juices flowing.

Use one of these Promises to develop your own Promise or go ahead and use one of these Promises exactly as we have written it. There are no extra style points for originality. Just make sure it moves you forward in your life and that you will be able to keep all of your Promises.

Gym Membership $40, Supplements $20, Special Cookbook $25 Losing Weight with The Promises Game = Priceless

PROMISE. MEAN IT. DO IT.

CHAPTER FOUR

YOUR FINANCES -
A PENNY SAVED IS A PENNY EARNED

"Here's our new retirement plan: at age 65,
we'll get divorced then marry other
people who planned better."

Every Promise you will make while playing The Promises Game can't be about weight loss (unless of course you're starring in a TV reality show about losing a lot of weight). For the rest of us, there are other areas of our lives that need attention. For many of us, that area is our finances. The Promises Game can help you earn more money, save more of the money that you earn and invest your savings wisely.

THE GREAT RECESSION OF 2008

The Great Recession of the last few years may have changed the American psyche for a generation. After two decades of free-spending and living beyond our means, Americans hit the spending brakes hard in 2008. Saving is suddenly very much in vogue. It remains to be seen whether this change will be permanent or whether we will return to our spendthrift ways after a brief penance. But one thing is certain, most of us look at our credit card debt differently than we did five years ago.

You Think We Have it Bad

Sally had the misfortune of turning 18 in the late fall of 1929. She also turned 30 on December 7, 1941. She always felt bad that her birthday had become a "day that would live in infamy." She came of age at the start of the Great Depression and proceeded to endure the next 16 years in times of severe financial austerity until the end of the Second World War. She lived into the 21st Century and remained frugal to her last days. She really knew the value of a dollar. We could all learn from her.

How has the Great Recession affected you? Is money tight? Are you worried about losing your job? Is your house worth half what it was worth five years ago? Even if you are doing well, are your neighbors in trouble? How about your friends and family? These are days when managing your finances is more important than ever.

MONEY, MONEY, MONEY

Finances cover a wide range of topics from making more money, to saving money and to investing wisely. At the risk of oversimplification, healthy finances come down to a single basic principle. With weight loss, the key is to consume fewer calories than you expend. With finances, you have to earn more money than you spend. Either increase your earnings or decrease your consumption; preferably, both.

Canning Vegetables

"My grandfather started his life off with fairly modest beginnings. I can remember the stories he would share about canning vegetables and preparing for the brutal winters of the Midwest. Later in his life he was very successful, but he never forgot the lessons of where he came from. He once told me that 'it's not how much money you make but rather how you manage the money that you have.' He managed his money *very* well and I will never forget this sound advice" *Christopher*

A really important tool for accomplishing many of these goals is creating and sticking to a budget. With The Promises Game you will be able to set new Promises to move yourself closer to your financial and budget goals. No matter where you

> *Chains of habits are too light to be felt until they are too heavy to be broken.*
>
> **—Warren Buffet**

are with your personal finances, you can always do something extra in your week to keep your financial house in order. It's not just the money you make, it's how you manage it. Making a simple Promise regarding finances each week can yield big results in the long run. Develop good financial habits not bad ones.

Here are some sample Promises related to your finances. We will start with 15 standard Promises, any one of which you could easily incorporate into a week. Revise them to reflect your exact circumstances, or take them verbatim from here.

 ## FIFTEEN STANDARD PROMISES

- I PROMISE TO FINISH AND FILE MY INCOME TAXES.

- I PROMISE TO WASH MY OWN CAR RATHER THAN GO TO A CAR WASH.

- I PROMISE TO BALANCE MY CHECKBOOK.

    Does anyone ever balance their checkbook anymore? It really is important, especially if you want to avoid those outrageous and expanding bank overdraft fees.

- I PROMISE TO KEEP A LEDGER OF MY SPENDING THIS WEEK.

    You may be surprised at the choices you will make when you know that you will be writing down those purchases. Maybe you won't buy a fourth set of commemorative Elvis plates on QVC this week.

- I PROMISE TO SHOP IN A THRIFT STORE.

    For some of us it took a recession to teach us that we can get a lot of good stuff at thrift stores if we are willing to look hard. Sometimes the hunt can be a lot of fun too. The key is to use your imagination. You don't have a marketing staff presenting everything in perfect lighting and dramatic organization. The perfect candlesticks for your dining room table might be found right next to a Hillbilly Bob 1988 coffee mug.

- I PROMISE TO SET UP AN APPOINTMENT WITH A FINANCIAL ADVISOR.

- I PROMISE TO USE THREE COUPONS THIS WEEK.

    Just make sure that you are buying something that you need and want. It doesn't save any money to get 25% off an item that you never should have bought in the first place.

- I PROMISE TO FIND AT LEAST THREE PRICES FOR THE NEW TELEVISION THAT I WANT TO BUY.

    For big ticket items like televisions, shop around for the best price. Go online and compare. Look for special deals and coupons.

- I PROMISE TO BUY A PERSONAL FINANCE BOOK AND START READING IT.

There's lots of great financial advisors out there, but one of the best for good advice and for putting money into its proper perspective is Suze Orman. She has shows on CNBC and her website is, not surprisingly, _suzeorman. com_. But, select whoever works for you. The key is to learn how to handle your money and then do it.

> *People first, then money, then things.*
>
> **—Suze Orman**

41

- I PROMISE TO ROLL UP ALL MY COINS AND TAKE THEM TO THE BANK.

  If you can, take them to the bank rather than one of those coin machines. The commissions can really take a chunk out of your efforts. Currently, it can be almost 10%. You sometimes can avoid the fee entirely if you accept a gift card from the merchant hosting the coin machine. If you shop there regularly anyway, that might be a good alternative. Otherwise go to the bank and save the 10%.

- I PROMISE TO SELECT FIVE BRAND-NAME GRO-CERY ITEMS THAT I OFTEN BUY AND INSTEAD PURCHASE EACH ONE'S GENERIC SUBSTITUTE.

  Generic brands are those brands that are not advertized but are usually shelved right next to or at least near the branded items. They are often much cheaper because they don't have to support ad campaigns. Their quality is often, but not always, equal to the branded versions. By trying out generic brands you can often find compa-rable quality for big savings. Some generic brands are even produced in the same factories as their branded counterparts. And yes sometimes they aren't very good, but you won't know until you try some out.

  "Some of the best beef jerky I have ever bought was the generic brand at one of the big chain stores. I go out of my way to get it there when I take a road trip. Nothing better than beef jerky for a long road trip."Valfrid

- I PROMISE TO SWITCH TO GENERIC BRANDS FOR DRUGS.

  Generic drugs (whether prescription or over the counter) are different from generic groceries. When a drug company creates a new drug they are granted a patent on that drug that gives them the exclusive right to sell it for about 20 years. If someone else tries to sell the exact same drug, at least in the United States, the drug company can sue and stop them. They have a monopoly on that drug. That's why new drugs can be very expensive. Once the drug goes "off-patent" competitors can sell that drug without having incurred the research costs. Verify that the generic brand of any name drug you are taking is exactly the same and if so, switch to it and save a lot of money.

- I PROMISE TO TAKE MY LUNCH TO WORK EACH DAY THIS WEEK.

    Those ten dollar salads can really add up over time. And they don't cost ten dollars to make at home.

FIVE QUICK OR TIME-CREATING PROMISES

- I PROMISE TO REPAY MY BROTHER THE $200 I BORROWED FROM HIM LAST YEAR.

    How many people have you lent money to, who have never paid you back? Don't be one of those people, if you can help it. At least acknowledge the debt and come up with some plan to pay it back. If you really don't have the money, maybe you can pay it off with work or in kind.

    Creditors have better memories than debtors.

    —Benjamin Franklin

- I PROMISE TO SEND IN A CHECK TO FUND MY IRA.

  An IRA is an Individual Retirement Account. These days most of you are responsible for your own retirement funds. No more regular pensions. If you don't have a 401(k) at work, you can put money aside in an IRA. You don't have to pay taxes on it until you withdraw it when you retire and the money earned in the account also isn't taxed until you withdraw it when you retire. Start as early as possible. You will probably need it.

- I PROMISE NOT TO GO TO THE MALL.

  You don't always have to Promise to do something. A negative Promise, like this one, is a Promise NOT to do something. And like so many negative Promises, you can't complain that you don't have enough time this week NOT to go shopping at the mall. For further discussion on negative Promises, check out Chapter Eleven.

- I PROMISE TO DONATE $50 TO A CHARITY.

  Giving back is a great way to get ahead financially. We believe in Karma.

- I PROMISE TO BUY REGULAR COFFEE AT STAR-BUCKS RATHER THAN A MORE EXPENSIVE FANCY COFFEE.

  Or better yet, brew it at home and take it with you. Prepare your coffeepot the night before and set the timer so that it's ready (and inexpensive) when you wake up.

FIVE CREATIVE PROMISES

- I PROMISE TO WORK THREE HOURS AT A SOUP KITCHEN.

> Giving back is a large part of being successful in this world. Giving back doesn't always require money, time works too. And we still believe in karma. We are at least idealistic enough to believe that helping others is a path to financial success in this world. Maybe not in a direct dollar for dollar basis, but it still seems to work somehow.

- I PROMISE TO CHECK OUT A BOOK FROM THE PUBLIC LIBRARY RATHER THAN BUY IT NEW.

> Or borrow a good book (or magazine) from a friend, especially a friend with similar interests. Don't most people have a dozen good books that they would love to recommend and loan to a friend? As an added bonus, you can talk about the book with your friend after you finish reading it. And please remember to return the book after you are finished. Or better yet, Promise to return it.

- I PROMISE TO REPLACE MY REGULAR LIGHT BULBS WITH ENERGY-SAVING LIGHT BULBS.

- I PROMISE TO MEMORIZE WHO IS ON EACH OF THE PAPER BILLS FROM THE $1 BILL THROUGH THE $100 BILL.

- I PROMISE TO SPEND ONLY *CASH* THIS WEEK FOR MY DAILY EXPENDITURES.

> Now this might seem a little odd at first glance and it might not be helpful for everyone, but hear us out.

When you play blackjack at a casino, you are required to convert your money into chips. There are obvious efficiencies involved in using standard chips rather than bills and coins that could easily be confused. However, one of the chief reasons the casino wants you to use innocent looking chips rather than $20 bills, is to obscure how much money you are really betting at any one time. You will spend more money at a casino the more you can be mentally divorced from the feeling that you are actually betting REAL money. The same holds true with our use of credit cards and debit cards. $50 on a debit card does not feel the same as two Andrew Jacksons (he's on the $20 bill) and an Alexander Hamilton (he's on the $10 bill). If you consistently find that you spend too much money each month on credit and debit cards, try paying with cash only. It will feel different and we think you will spend less naturally. This won't work for everyone, but it will work for some of you.

There are a lot of good Promises that you can make concerning your finances. Whether you are looking to make more money, spend less, save more or just get some good karma, it's all here. And as always, adapt your Promises to your unique situation. Or make your Promise exactly as we wrote it above. Whatever works for you.

The Promises Game is not a get-rich-quick scheme. Playing The Promises Game will not cause the stocks you buy to skyrocket. It won't keep your house from losing 50% of its value in a real estate downturn. If things are going well, The Promises Game will help maximize your success. However, if life deals you a tough hand, The Promises Game will give you the ability to weather the storm and be prepared to take advantage of the next opportunity.

PROMISE. MEAN IT. DO IT.

CHAPTER FIVE

HABITS - THE GOOD, THE BAD AND THE RUTS

Copyright 2002 by Randy Glasbergen.   www.glasbergen.com

This chapter is about habits. You will learn how to use The Promises Game to break or moderate bad habits as well as create new good habits. Here we will introduce the concept of consistency. You can use consistency along with accountability to break or moderate bad habits as well as create new good habits. You will need to repeat Promises over a period of several weeks to eliminate a bad habit or establish a new good habit. You are your habits; are your habits working for you?

> *The second half of a man's life is made up of nothing but the habits he has acquired during the first half.*
>
> **—Feodor Dostoevsky**

We are creature of habits. The Oxford Dictionary defines a habit as "A settled disposition or tendency to act in a certain way, especially one acquired by frequent repetition of the same act until it is almost involuntary." Habits can be good, bad or neutral. Without habits, life would be much more difficult. Imagine if you needed to deal with each situation that you encounter in life as if you had never experienced it before. Habit allows you to apply your past experiences to a current situation and use previously successful actions and reactions to deal with what is happening to you in the present. If these actions occur on a regular basis, we call these actions habits.

HABITS

If under stress you smoke a cigarette, that action would be considered a habit. If you like to have a cup of coffee when you are tired, that might be considered a habit.

> *Men's natures are alike; it is their habits that separate them.*
>
> **—Confucius**

If you always go for a walk when you are suffering from writer's block, that might be considered a habit. If you brush your teeth every night before you go to bed, that would be considered a habit.

In each instance there is a situation and a conscious reaction. Here we are only dealing with conscious actions, although subconscious actions (e.g., getting an upset stomach when you are very nervous) and involuntary actions (e.g., blinking your eyes when a bright light is shined on your face) can be very important as well in our lives.

Whether the reaction constitutes a habit is a matter of frequency. For example, if you are about to go to bed and decide to brush your teeth, it is a reaction not a habit if you only do so on a sporadic basis. If you always or almost always brush your teeth before you go to bed, it would be a habit. How can The Promises Game help you deal with your conscious habits?

TYPES OF HABITS

We separate conscious habits into three main categories - good habits, good habits if in moderation and bad habits. Whether a habit is good, good in moderation or bad is often subjective. Most people would agree that brushing your teeth every night before going to bed is a good habit. Many people would assert that having five cigarettes every time you are anxious is a bad habit. But some people believe that having one cigarette while having a drink is an acceptable reaction to a situation. It is not our goal to decide whether a certain reaction to a situation is or is not a habit. Nor is it our intent to determine whether a habit or reaction is 'good,' "acceptable in moderation" or 'bad.' If you decide that smoking cigarettes is a bad habit for you, we will show you how The Promises Game can help you accomplish your desire of stopping smoking. If you decide that three cups of coffee a day is immoderate and want to limit yourself to two cups a day, The Promises Game can help you achieve that purpose. If you decide that you want to floss your teeth every day after eating breakfast, The Promises Game can help.

BAD HABITS (AND WE DON'T MEAN ILL-FITTING HATS FOR NUNS)

The Promises Game is well suited for what we would more classically call bad habits. Bad habits are anything that you do on a consistent basis that you do not want to continue doing. You should be able to conquer most bad habits in three to four months, about how long it takes to play The Promises Game. Some bad habits may need to be stopped completely while others may only be a problem because you engage in them to excess. For example, you might feel that drinking five sodas a day is a bad habit, but one soda a day would be fine. Promises related to habits both good and bad are often Promises that you might want to repeat for successive weeks. You will need to develop consistency. If your goal is to quit smoking, you probably will not accomplish your goal in one week. Additionally you may prefer to gradually decrease a bad habit. For example, in the first week, you might choose to limit yourself to no more than five cigarettes per day. In the next week you might choose to reduce that limitation to four. You would continue this regression until you reached the level that you sought, whether that is zero per day or some other number that you decide is appropriate for you. Others might feel that they need to stop smoking cold turkey, perhaps with the benefit of some prescription drug or an over the counter aid like nicotine gum. Whatever method you chose can be incorporated into The Promises Game.

> *The unfortunate thing about this world is that good habits are so much easier to give up than bad ones.*
>
> **—W. Somerset Maugham**

Other bad habits could be dealt with in a similar fashion. The first week you might Promise to watch no more than two hours of TV each day. The next week you might reduce that limit to 90 minutes. Eventually you would reach your desired level. If after a few weeks of eliminating a bad habit you find that it has crept back into your life, go ahead and make the Promise once more, or even the start the regression process again.

Promises related to bad habits are not limited to merely cutting down on the quantity of a bad habit. For more serious issues, your Promise might be to visit your doctor to discuss potential drugs to help you quit smoking. You might want to Promise to attend an AA meeting or get a sponsor if alcohol or drug abuse is a concern for you. Nevertheless, Promises regarding bad habits are more likely to be negative Promises (that is a Promise not to do something bad) rather than an affirmative Promise (that is a Promise to do something good).

GOOD HABITS

The Promises Game works equally well for developing good habits. Sometimes, of course, creating a good habit is a two-step process. First you need to overcome or at least moderate a bad habit and then you need to create the new good habit to fill the void. For example, you might want to stop watching too much TV and replace it with reading books on a regular basis. Or maybe you go shopping when you are bored. Why not instead garden, hike or play tennis. Success in overcoming the bad habit is partially dependent upon providing an alternate activity to replace it.

We have seen a lot of discussion on how long it takes to establish a new good habit. We have seen everything from three weeks to three months. Chances are there is no magic number. Some good habits probably take longer to establish than others. Also if you are simultaneously trying to eliminate a bad habit, it will take longer to complete both parts of the process. Three weeks to 30 days seems to be the quickest you can establish a new good habit. With The Promises Game, the key may be to repeat a Promise to do something that you want to make a habit for three, four or even more weeks in a row. If you establish a good habit by making it a Promise for four straight weeks you could drop it as a Promise. However, if you stop keeping that good habit, you can make it a Promise again for a week or two to reestablish the good habit. Consistency and accountability are the keys.

Making the Dentist Happy

Justin used The Promises Game to establish very consistent brushing and flossing habits. As a result he has had perfect dental check-ups for several years. He no longer needs to Promise to brush or floss anymore. It is a solid good habit. On the other hand, no matter how hard he tries, Justin rarely can get himself to write in his journal unless he makes it a Promise.

RUT-BUSTERS

Rut-Busters are a special form of Promise that we developed a few years back. A rut is something that you do on a regular basis that neither constitutes a good nor a bad habit. It is neutral, even possibly slightly good. But you almost always do the same thing, the same way, even when other alternatives are available. Flossing your teeth every day is a good habit. Biting your fingernails too short when you are anxious is a bad habit. Going to the same two restaurants for lunch almost every business day is probably a rut, even if they are good and well-priced.

How would we define a rut? Well frankly it is different for every person. Justice Potter Stewart of the U.S. Supreme Court in 1964, in an attempt to define pornography said he couldn't define pornography, "but I know it when I see it." Some people just feel comfortable with their routines. If that's you, skip this section. But we think that most people end up doing the same comfortable things for no good reason. If you want to practice breaking out of ruts, here's a Promise for you - I Promise to do five things differently this week. That is to say, I Promise to do five rut-busters this week. You can leave it this general or you can actually list out the ruts that you want to break this week. You don't have to change every instance of a rut, just some of them.

The only result of trying a rut-buster may be that you agree that the way you did something before really is the best way to do something. That's a-ok. Or you may discover something new and better. Or maybe you'll just add some variety to spice up your life. We Promise you, however, that keeping an open mind to doing things in a different way will greatly expand your life. Use the rut-busters Promise to help learn this trick. Here are some suggestions for "ruts" to "bust":

-Eat lunch at different places rather than your usual two.

-Eat three meals with your left hand (if you are right-handed).

> There is some evidence that doing things differently, such as eating with your left hand (if you're right-handed) actually builds new connections in your brain.

-Drive a different route to work each day.

-Change sides of the bed with your partner three nights this week.

-Drink 1% fat milk this week instead of 2%.

-Read the front page of the newspaper before the sports page.

-Eat breakfast in the dining room instead of in front of the TV.

-Walk the dog in the morning rather than the evening.

-Drink Pepsi rather than Coke.

-Use a different shade of lipstick two times this week.

-Wear a different pair of shoes each day this week.

These are some specific examples of rut-busters. You could make any one of these a separate Promise, but unless the rut is a very big problem or you are having a very busy week, we would lump three to five of these into one large rut-buster Promise. The key to the rut-buster Promise is to do several things differently this week to create a new mindset that, hopefully, will spill over into other areas of your life. You are just trying to break out of ruts and see the world from a different point of view.

We have fewer comments on these sample Promises. Many of these Promises, especially in the Standard Promises section, are self-explanatory.

 ## FIFTEEN STANDARD PROMISES

- I PROMISE TO FLOSS MY TEETH EVERYDAY.

    An invaluable habit to develop.

- I PROMISE NOT TO GO TO A FAST FOOD RESTAURANT.

- I PROMISE ONLY TO DRINK ALCOHOL ON SATURDAY NIGHT.

- I PROMISE TO TALK TO MY DOCTOR ABOUT PRESCIPTION DRUGS TO HELP STOP SMOKING.

- I PROMISE NOT TO EAT ANY CANDY.

    Make sure you are clear in your mind about what constitutes candy. Would substituting cookies or doughnuts be consistent with this Promise to you?

- I PROMISE NOT TO EAT AFTER 9:00 PM EACH NIGHT.

    Many people believe that late night eating leads to unwanted weight gain. If you agree, this Promise may be for you.

- I PROMISE TO WRITE IN MY JOURNAL FOUR TIMES THIS WEEK.

- I PROMISE TO READ FROM THE BIBLE AT LEAST TEN MINUTES EACH DAY.

- I PROMISE TO DRINK TWO LITERS OF WATER DAILY.

- I PROMISE NOT TO DRINK ANY SODA.

- I PROMISE TO GET TO BED BY 10:00 P.M. BEFORE EACH WORKDAY.

- I PROMISE TO MAKE MY BED EACH MORNING BEFORE LEAVING THE HOUSE.

- I PROMISE NOT TO SWEAR IN FRONT OF MY KIDS.

- I PROMISE TO WRITE IN MY JOURNAL DAILY.

- I PROMISE TO FINISH ALL MY LAUNDRY BY FRIDAY.

FIVE QUICK OR TIME-CREATING PROMISES

- I PROMISE TO WATCH NO MORE THAN ONE HOUR OF TV PER DAY.

    Probably the ultimate time-saving Promise (right after watching no TV). No one doesn't have enough time to watch less TV. If your Promises Partner complains that he doesn't have enough time to make and keep Promises, pull out this Promise.

- I PROMISE TO DRINK ONLY DECAF COFFEE.

  Good and bad habits are an area that is full of quick and time-creating Promises. On those weeks where you are really pressed for time, come to this chapter on habits. It would be acceptable to select all of your Promises from this area, if necessary.

- I PROMISE NOT TO CRITICIZE MY HUSBAND'S DRIVING.

  Or not to criticize your wife's cooking. Or not to criticize your son's messiness. Constant criticism is a bad habit too.

- I PROMISE TO TAKE A MULTI-VITAMIN ONCE A DAY WITH BREAKFAST.

- I PROMISE NOT TO SMOKE THIS WEEK.

 ## FIVE CREATIVE PROMISES

- I PROMISE TO COMPLETE FIVE RUT-BUSTERS THIS WEEK.

  See the discussion above about rut-busters.

- I PROMISE TO COMPLIMENT THREE DIFFERENT PEOPLE EVERY DAY.

  This can be harder than you think unless you have already made a habit of being complimentary. This could be just three different people each day, or be more aggressive and make it 21 different people (that's three different people seven straight days).

- I PROMISE TO SMILE AT THREE STRANGERS EACH DAY.

- I PROMISE TO DO 100 SIT-UPS OR PUSHUPS EACH TIME I SMOKE A CIGARETTE.

  You'll either get washboard abs or decide smoking isn't worth it.

- I PROMISE A MYSTERY PROMISE.

  Sometimes Promises in the area of habits, especially bad habits, end up being mystery Promises. You might be uncomfortable discussing some of your more embarrassing shortcomings with your Promises Partner. Don't let this hold you back if conquering the habit is important to you. Use the mystery Promise to deal with this issue. See Chapter Two for more information on mystery Promises.

The Promises Game is uniquely effective at conquering bad habits. It is also just as good at creating good habits. Use it for both types of habits. You will probably want to repeat important Promises for several weeks until you are sure you have eliminated the bad habit or formed the new good habit. A 30-day time span is a good rule of thumb; but take whatever time is enough for you.

PROMISE. MEAN IT. DO IT.

CHAPTER SIX

THERE'S NO PLACE LIKE HOME

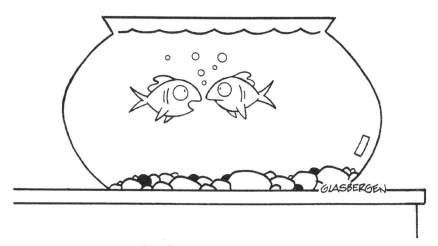

© Randy Glasbergen
www.glasbergen.com

"It's not bad for our first home. You'll like it better
after I add a fireplace, more closets, and a deck."

Whether you live in a studio apartment in Brooklyn, a bungalow in the suburbs of Los Angeles or a sprawling ranch in Montana, there are many things that you may want or need to do in and around your home. We look at what you do around your home from two perspectives. The first perspective is what you do to clean and maintain your home. The second is what you do to make your home aesthetically pleasing and to reflect your personality.

You probably spend over half of your life at home. There are things you need to do regularly to maintain your home in a sanitary and efficient state. That's called cleaning. Mom tried to teach us to clean, but not all moms succeeded. Some of us needed to suffer the consequences of living in our own mess for a while until we learned to clean or got a cleaning service. We would include maintenance in the broad category of cleaning. Maintenance is basically fixing things that go wrong, either before (if you're lucky or smart) or after they break or wear down.

If you own your own home, you don't have a landlord to turn to, so the amount of things that need to be done around the house can really build up. Even a renter will need to keep their home clean and well-decorated. Since everyone needs to keep their home or apartment clean, whether they pay rent or make a mortgage payment (or live with their parents) let's start there.

ASK THE EXPERTS

If you want to improve an area in your life, it's a good idea to go to the experts for help and guidance.

Making Mom Happy

Robert was never able to clean his home. It seemed that no matter how hard he tried, cleaning never even approached the quality of his mother's efforts. She would probably be surprised that he could even muster up any cleaning abilities. As a teenager he was very messy. We will spare you the stories of bubble-gum on the headboards, piles of dirty laundry and rotting food under the bed. Anyone with teenagers knows what we are talking about. That was Robert. And he wasn't much better after college.

The only reasonable solution was to get a cleaning service, an extravagance he indulged for several years. This made more sense when he was a busy professional making a comfortable salary. Eventually though, in tighter economic times, he decided that he needed to handle the cleaning himself. He discovered a great series of books by Jeff Campbell and the Clean Team. The lead book in the series is entitled *Speed Cleaning.* He used The Promises Game to implement the book. *Speed Cleaning* sets forth an organized system of weekly cleaning that makes keeping your home clean and tidy a breeze. Cleaning can be almost fun. When Robert's kitchen and bathroom looked as good as his Mom's, Robert had a tremendous sense of satisfaction.

© 1998 Randy Glasbergen.

**"I'm the Clutter Fairy. I'll come back...
I'm gonna need a much bigger wand!"**

We agree with Robert, *Speed Cleaning* is a great book on cleaning. We have read numerous cleaning-related books. The others didn't necessarily work for us, perhaps because we experienced them at the wrong time in our lives or because we were not using The Promises Game to implement our reading. This one worked for us too, so it is the one that we usually recommend to our Promise Partners when they mention cleaning as a priority for them. But feel free to use your own cleaning system or the system that your Mom or Dad taught you. The Promises Game book is not a review of great ideas on different subjects, but, when we have something that we especially like, that has worked well for us, we will bring it up. On our website, ThePromisesGame.org, we will provide you opportunities to recommend your own favorite books and suggestions in any areas of your lives that might involve Promises.

> *Cleaning your house while your kids are still growing is like shoveling the walk before it stops snowing.*
>
> **—Phyllis Diller**

THE JOY OF CLEANING

You will be surprised at the satisfaction that you can experience from a thorough cleaning of your house or apartment. It is strangely fulfilling, especially if you're not used to it. Sometimes when you are feeling down or in a rut, just start cleaning the house or a part of the house, no matter how small and you may find that a clean kitchen is all that you need to take on your taxes this afternoon. Often times we just need the momentum of tackling a small project to get us up to speed for tackling

> *Housework is something that you do that nobody notices until you don't do it.*
>
> **—Anonymous**

larger projects. When you can't seem to accomplish anything else, at least doing the dishes is something.

DECORATING AND REMODELING

Living in a clean and orderly place is great, heck it's next to Godliness, but you also want your place to be beautiful and charming and reflect your personality and taste. This is decorating and remodeling.

> *Creativity is allowing yourself to make mistakes. Design is knowing which ones to keep.*
>
> **—Scott Adams**

The first decade of the 21st Century (will we ever decide what name to give that decade?), in addition to witnessing one of the greatest housing bubbles ever seen in America, also included an enormous boom in home remodeling. Millions got excited about making the homes they lived in bigger and better than before, whether the intent was for resale or personal enjoyment. Television shows like "Designed to Sell" and "Curb Appeal," as well as entire cable networks, like Home and Garden TV (HGTV) quickly grew in popularity and before we knew it our prime time favorites included a show about remodeling our home, reorganizing a cluttered apartment and oriental landscaping.

So here are some possible Promises you could make regarding cleaning your home and decorating (or remodeling) your living space. We will start with 15 standard promises. By that we mean simple straight-forward Promises that you can use as is or modify to fit your own circumstances.

FIFTEEN STANDARD PROMISES

- I PROMISE TO DO ALL THE DISHES EVERY NIGHT BEFORE I GO TO BED.

   This can be hard, especially if you are tired, but it feels great to wake up to a clean kitchen.

- I PROMISE TO CLEAN THE BATHROOM.

   See the comments on *Speed Cleaning* above. It's actually possible to clean a toilet in under two minutes.

- I PROMISE TO SPRING CLEAN THE BATHROOM.

   By spring clean, rather than clean, we mean that kind of thorough deep cleaning that you might only do a couple times a year. You move furniture, scour the corners and maybe toss out old items that you don't need any more. And no, you don't need to wait until spring.

- I PROMISE TO MAKE MY BED EVERY MORNING BEFORE I GO TO WORK

- I PROMISE TO SWEEP AND HOSE DOWN THE DRIVEWAY.

- I PROMISE TO MAKE AN APPOINTMENT WITH AN ELECTRICIAN TO COME AND FIX THE PORCH LIGHTS.

   You don't have to do the work yourself, just so long as it gets done. Knowing what you don't know is as important as knowing how to do it yourself.

- I PROMISE TO CLEAN OUT THE REFRIGERATOR.

    This needs to be done much more often than you usually do it. Not only will you get rid of overripe produce, but you might find things in the back that are still quite usable. You will also find that it gets easier every time you do it. For us it only took a couple months until it was part of our routine and usually got done by the time a pot of water reached its boiling point.

- I PROMISE TO REPAIR THE LEAKY FAUCET IN THE GUEST BATHROOM.

    Repairing broken or worn out items is as important as cleaning.

- I PROMISE TO WASH ALL THE WINDOWS IN THE HOUSE.

    This is one of the hardest cleaning chores. There's a reason some maids won't do windows? Anyone who has an easy, efficient way to clean windows, please let us know. That being said, a quick clean with a couple of streaks beats dirty windows any day.

- I PROMISE TO MOW THE LAWN.

- I PROMISE TO CLEAN OUT THE RAIN GUTTERS.

    Is there a more unpleasant chore that you know you have to accomplish, but put off and put off until it becomes a real problem. Make it a Promise and it will get done - this week - before it's too late!

- I PROMISE TO WEED THE FLOWER BEDS.

    This is another tedious chore that really isn't that hard, but just doesn't seem to happen as often as it should. Make it a Promise and it will get done - this week! You may even find that you enjoy the time getting your hands dirty.

- I PROMISE TO FIX THE BROKEN CABINET DOOR.

    Remember, you are Promising that the cabinet door will get fixed, no one said you had to do it alone. You can always delegate a Promise out to your kids, significant other or a handy man. Be prepared to step in and do it yourself if it looks like it's not going to get done. "My son forgot to do it" won't fly as a valid excuse at your next Promises Meeting.

- I PROMISE TO REORGANIZE MY SPICES TO MAKE THEM MORE ACCESSIBLE.

    But please don't alphabetize them. That's just too much. The problem with spices is that they are often crowded in a cupboard and you don't remember what spices you have or what's still fresh. Spices don't stay fresh forever, replace them occasionally. And if you want to alphabetize them, go ahead, just don't tell anyone.

- I PROMISE TO ORDER A NEW COUCH FOR THE LIVING ROOM.

    Brand new quality furniture sometimes needs to be ordered weeks even months in advance. So take that into account.

- I PROMISE TO SIGN UP FOR A COURSE ON INTERIOR DECORATING AT THE LOCAL COMMUNITY COLLEGE.

    If not a full course, how about a Saturday afternoon seminar often available at large stores. They have repair and special do-it-yourself classes as well. Some are pretty good. And you usually don't need to sign up in advance, just show up. They want to sell you more hardware and supplies, so it's in their best interests to get you excited about home improvement projects.

- I PROMISE TO WATCH A TV SHOW ON REMODELING.

  Or watch a Youtube clip or similar video online about remodeling or decorating.

- I PROMISE TO PAINT THE BABY'S ROOM THIS WEEKEND.

  Hopefully, you have done your research before making this Promise. Nontoxic, child-safe paint can be a little more pricey and you'll want to make sure you have purchased the necessary supplies first. If you have not done this then you could always make it your Promise to do so.

- I PROMISE TO FIND A NEW VASE FOR THE END TABLE AND SPEND LESS THAN $10.

  Check out the thrift and second-hand stores. They can provide a lot of variety and are much cheaper. Try to look at a potential vase out of the context of all the other stuff around it in the thrift store. Thrift stores don't create the same sales presentation that a full-service mall store does. But if you use your imagination, you can get the same quality vase at a fraction of the price. Also Craigslist and eBay are other great places to find bargains. Make a game of it. Or better yet, make it a Promise.

FIVE QUICK OR TIME-CREATING PROMISES

These are five Promises related to your house that either don't require any meaningful amount of time expenditure or even create more time in your week. You can't complain that you don't have enough time in the week to keep these Promises.

- I PROMISE TO ASK MY HUSBAND TO DO THE DISHES THIS WEEK.

  > Assuming your husband is cooperative, this will free up some time for you to work on other Promises or other things that need to be done. Hopefully, you won't have to redo the dishes afterwards. If so, maybe a future Promise (when you have more time available) would be to train your husband to do the dishes. Good luck.

- I PROMISE TO ASK EVERYONE IN THE HOUSE TO WRITE DOWN THE THREE CHORES THEY WOULD MOST LIKE TO DO.

  > This will give them the illusion that they have a choice in the matter (insert maniacal laugh here). But in all seriousness this is a great way to get the family involved and to help ease the challenges that may come from delegating chores around the house.

- I PROMISE TO HAVE THE NEIGHBOR BOY MOW MY YARD.

  > Note the common thread here is having someone else do something that needs to be done around your house. It may cost you some money, but it will save you a lot of time.

- I PROMISE TO PUT MY DIRTY CLOTHES DIRECTLY INTO THE HAMPER RATHER THAN ON THE FLOOR.

  > You can't complain that you don't have enough time to do this. Put the hamper next to your bed if you have to.

- I PROMISE TO GET RID OF FIVE ITEMS AROUND THE HOUSE THAT I NO LONGER LIKE OR NEED.

  An integral part of cleaning and remodeling is getting rid of what isn't working.

- I PROMISE TO ???

  We really wanted to come up with more legitimate quick Promises regarding remodeling, but we couldn't. It just plain takes a lot of time to decorate and remodel your house. If you're short on time in any given week, select your Promises from other areas of your life.

FIVE CREATIVE PROMISES

- I PROMISE TO MAKE A REMODELING VISION BOARD.

  A vision board can be as simple as gluing a bunch of clippings from a magazine on to a poster board. These pictures represent the image you wish to create and present a vision of how you wish to see your home one day. Have fun with this one. Finally a use for all of those *Architectural Digests* that you have been saving in the garage!

- I PROMISE TO THROW AN "I-CAN'T-AFFORD-A-DECORATOR" PARTY.

  "I moved back to Los Angeles from Seattle in 2000. I bought a house that definitely would need a lot of remodeling and decorating. I didn't want to hire a decorator, but needed some help. I had a lot of very creative friends, so I threw a party at my new house and asked everyone to give me ideas on what to do. I especially paid attention to the comments from people who had homes that I really liked. I got many good ideas and used a lot of them. The house turned out great. I call this an 'I-can't-afford-a-decorator' party." *Valfrid*

- I PROMISE TO WRITE DOWN "WHAT WOULD MICHELLE DO?" AND PLACE IT IN THE AREA I WISH TO REMODEL.

  "Michelle is a good friend and an interior decorator that I know. I love her taste and choices in design. She once visited a small studio apartment I had recently moved into and saw that most of my things were either still in boxes or strewn about in no real order. While I was heating up some tea she moved a few items around and hung a couple of pieces of art that I had. By the time our visit was over my barren bachelor pad had the feeling of a warm inviting home. Although I would love to hire her for all my design choices, some things we just need to do on our own. My design decisions aren't always the best but by thinking about the way she designs I can get out of my own way and make some pretty good choices." *Christopher*

- I PROMISE TO THROW A DINNER PARTY THIS WEEK.

  Throwing a dinner party is the sure-fire way to get your house clean. And fast!

- I PROMISE TO TAKE A FULL SET OF *BEFORE* PICTURES OF THE HOUSE.

We so wish we had taken our own advice here, but we never did and we regret it. Learn from our mistakes.

You probably don't need a lot of creativity in deciding Promises to make in cleaning your house. If you are really challenged, get a book on cleaning or organizing. If you need a suggestion on a specific cleaning Promise, just walk around your home and look at what needs to be done. If you are short on time, but still want to clean something, pick something small. Decorating and remodeling probably require more forethought and time.

PROMISE. MEAN IT. DO IT.

SOME QUESTIONS

We would like to take a short break and address a few questions that may have arisen. A couple are directly related to this chapter and a few are more general questions.

1. Why do so many of the Promises in the chapter seem mundane and ordinary. I thought The Promises Game was about accomplishing big things?

> There are many nuanced levels to The Promises Game. You can accomplish great things using the game, especially stringing together related Promises over several weeks. The Promises Game is also about learning to keep your Promises and learning how to make good Promises. And finally it's about getting things done that just don't get done. This chapter lent itself to that final level of getting things done that just plain need to be done.

2. What if I make a Promise but I want to change my mind in the middle of the week?

> This will happen. Sometimes you will have something that you want to achieve and you make it a Promise. As your week progresses, you discover that another Promise would work better, makes more sense or simply that you made a bad Promise. This will be part of your learning process in the game. Once a Promise is made there is no turning back. Your obligation remains the same, keep your Promise. The next week you will have the opportunity to really evaluate your Promises and see if there is a way you can avoid running into the same circumstances that led to your desire to change course.

3. If I Promise to clean the bathroom and finish the project early in the week, does it matter if the bathroom is dirty again at the end of the week?

Everyone's Promises are unique to themselves. You can make them what you want them to be, just be clear what you intend at the time you make the Promise. If your purpose in Promising to clean the bathroom was to do regular once-a-week cleaning, it wouldn't matter that the bathroom was not still clean at the end of the week, so long as it was cleaned once, *in excellence*. If on the other hand, you want the Promise to be "keep the bathroom clean," it needs to still be clean at the end of the week.

4. What do we do if we don't keep all of our Promises on the second round of ten Promises?

> If you fail on the second or third week of ten Promises you start over on the first week of ten Promises. If you fail on the first week of ten Promises, you go back to nine Promises.

5. Can you lose The Promises Game?

> The only way to lose The Promises Game is to quit.

CHAPTER SEVEN

THE PROMISING GOURMET

"My dog ate my homework — nobody else would!"

Over the last decade if Americans weren't trying to lose weight or remodeling their homes, they were learning to cook. Cooking became a competitive sport, even a contact sport at times. Chefs became celebrities in their own right. *The Food Network*, *The Cooking Channel* and hundreds of magazines and websites dedicated to cooking sprung up and flourished in the last dozen years. Farmers' markets with their abundant fresh produce in season are packed from coast to coast. In these harder financial times people wanted food that cost less, tasted better and was healthier. But most of all, a lot of us wanted to learn how to cook.

> *The only time to eat diet food is while you're waiting for the steak to cook.*
>
> **—Julia Child**

Learning to Cook

Donna has a large collection of cookbooks, some great, some good, some way over her head. There is only one book that she recommends for learning how to cook (although there are many good books out there). If you simply don't know how to cook she recommends *Cooking for Dummies* by Bryan Miller and Marie Rama. It is filled with recipes, but its purpose is to take you step by step through all the cooking basics from boiling and poaching through sauces to roasting a turkey. Over several months, using The Promises Game, she went chapter by chapter doing almost every single recipe. The book uses actual recipes to teach the various cooking techniques. Donna's copy is so used that it is falling apart and is covered with sauce splatters. She has become a decent everyday cook, not a gourmet chef; although she is working towards that.

Ethnic Cooking

Sometimes people want to learn more or master a specific style of cooking, such as Italian or Thai. Maybe they simply like a certain style of food. Or perhaps it represents their heritage. Mastering a style of food isn't going to happen in a single week. But over a number of weeks by making Promises to attend classes, read cookbooks and actually prepare dishes you can become the specialty chef you want to be.

Cooking your Heritage

Yao-Tung came to America from Taiwan when he was four years old. His family moved to Monterey Park just outside of Los Angeles, where they ran a Chinese restaurant. In spite of his family business, Yao-Tung never learned how to cook authentic Chinese food. In his early 30s, he decided that he really wanted to honor his heritage by learning to cook authentic Chinese cuisine. He used The Promises Game to rediscover his culinary heritage. He got several Chinese cookbooks, took a few seminars and practiced numerous recipes. In the end, he made a full Chinese dinner for his family. They were impressed.

So whatever your reason is for wanting to learn how to cook or to become a better cook, here are 15 standard Promises you can make to start you on the path towards being the next celebrity chef (or at least impress your guests at your next dinner party).

FIFTEEN STANDARD PROMISES

- I PROMISE TO COOK A ROMANTIC DINNER FOR MY GIRLFRIEND.

- I PROMISE TO COOK TWO NEW RECIPES.

> *Learn how to cook – try new recipes, learn from your mistakes, be fearless, and above all have fun!*
>
> **—Julia Child**

Select some dishes you really like to eat in a restaurant or from a new cookbook and try two out at home. If you are new to cooking, it's fine to start simple. Wolfgang Puck did not become a star chef in a week.

- I PROMISE TO BUY A NEW SET OF QUALITY KNIVES.

Probably a good cook's best friends.

- I PROMISE TO BUY A NEW COOKBOOK ON ITALIAN COOKING.

Check out used book stores and thrift stores. Cookbooks don't really get out-of-date. You can pick up great cookbooks at a fraction of the new book price.

- I PROMISE TO START AN HERB GARDEN.

Or a vegetable garden. Or even a couple of plants in the window or the patio planter. It always tastes better if you grow it yourself.

- I PROMISE TO RESEARCH FOOD PROCESSORS FOR PRICE AND QUALITY AND BUY ONE.

- I PROMISE TO MAKE MY LUNCH EACH DAY FOR WORK.

- I PROMISE TO GIVE MY POTS AND PANS A GOOD CLEANING.

  > Over time your pots and pans can accumulate a lot of crud that's hard to get off. It just feels better to cook with clean tools. The same applies to your appliances that can really get dirty. If something just can't be cleaned, maybe it's time for a replacement if the budget can handle it. This could be a guy thing.

- I PROMISE TO BAKE MY GRANDMA'S SPECIAL APPLE PIE.

- I PROMISE TO BUY A NEW BLENDER.

- I PROMISE TO GO TO THE FARMERS' MARKET TO GET FRESH PRODUCE.

- I PROMISE TO SHARPEN ALL OF MY KNIVES.

  > You can't be a good cook without sharp knives.

- I PROMISE TO BUY NEW SPICES TO REPLACE SPICES THAT ARE OVER ONE YEAR OLD.

  > Those rarely used spices can sit in the cupboard for a long time past their prime. But don't replace ones that you probably won't use. Save money by keeping the old containers and refilling them with spices from packets - much cheaper.

- I PROMISE TO COOK SOMETHING FROM SCRATCH THAT I HAVE NEVER COOKED BEFORE.

  > It doesn't have to be difficult, just a first for you. Maybe bake your first loaf of bread. How about spaghetti sauce from scratch. A batch of chocolate chip

cookies. If you haven't done it before use a recipe or even better watch a video on the internet on how to prepare what you are choosing to do for the first time.

- I PROMISE TO WATCH FIVE VIDEOS FROM A FOOD VIDEO BLOG AND TRY ONE OF THE RECIPES.

  Our favorite is foodwishes.com. Chef John walks you through a simple but creative recipe using a single camera angle focused not on the cook but on the food and the preparation. The video comes with the written recipe and comments, but the brilliance is in the video. He makes everything look so easy.

  FOODWISHES.COM

FIVE QUICK OR TIME-CREATING PROMISES

- I PROMISE TO PREPARE THREE CASSEROLES THIS WEEKEND AND FREEZE THEM TO HEAT UP FOR MEALS THROUGHOUT THE WEEK.

  This is a great way to save time over the course of the week. It doesn't take much longer to make a large batch of something than just a regular batch. Just make sure it's something that you want to eat more than once in a week. The fourth time in a row that you sit down to eat meatloaf might be two times too many.

- I PROMISE TO TRY A NEW ITEM ON THE MENU AT A RESTAURANT THAT I FREQUENT.

- I PROMISE TO USE UP OR TOSS OUT ALL OF THE LEFTOVERS IN THE REFRIGERATOR BEFORE COOKING ANYTHING NEW.

    A simple way to do this would be as you're stocking the fridge with fresh produce or new leftovers simply make room by tossing out the old stuff.

- I PROMISE TO MAKE MY OWN CRÈME FRAICHE FROM SCRATCH.

    Now this doesn't look like a quick Promise. Crème fraiche is basically French sour cream and it is wonderful. You would use it any time you might otherwise use sour cream and especially in white sauces for dishes like Fettuccini Alfredo or Beef Stroganoff. It has a richer almost nutty taste. It is the easiest thing you will ever make and it's very impressive. Get two cups of heavy cream (not ultra-pasteurized) and three tablespoons of cultured buttermilk. You don't need to heat the mixture. Combine in a partially open jar and leave at warm room temperature (75 degrees) for 24 hours. Then tighten the lid on the jar, and place in refrigerator for 24 hours. Voilá! You will have crème fraiche that should last up to two weeks. No work at all.

- I PROMISE TO ASK AUNT MARIA TO SEND ME HER APPLE STREUDEL RECIPE.

FIVE CREATIVE PROMISES

- I PROMISE TO START MY OWN PERSONAL RECIPE BOOK.

Gather two dozen of your favorite recipes that are easy to make and healthy. Perhaps retype them with your personal variations and comments and arrange them in a splatter-protected binder. As you cook them over and over you will get better and better at making them. In addition, you will get familiar with the ingredients that you need for these recipes and can stock up on them on the cheap when they go on sale or by buying in bulk, where practical, at a warehouse store.

"A couple of my nieces asked for copies of my personal recipes book when they went off to college." *Valfrid*

- I PROMISE TO EAT OUT AT A NEW RESTAURANT THAT I HAVE NEVER TRIED BEFORE.

  Assuming that you plan to eat out anyway, why not pick a restaurant you have never tried before. Maybe try an ethnic food that you've never had.

  Jason once made it a quest to find the perfect barbeque. He made the search several Promises over the course of a few weeks. Living in Los Angeles, he had a lot of choices. He tried everything from Brazilian, Armenian, Mongolian, Argentine, Korean, Southern and Texan. He tried charcoal-grilled, mesquite-grilled, smoked over a wood fire, cooked on stones and slow roasted in a special fire pit. He couldn't say which one was the absolute best, each had its own unique style and taste but he said that Brazilians definitely take their barbeque seriously and it shows.

- I PROMISE TO USE UP ALL THE LEFTOVER VEGETABLES AND MAKE STOCK WITH THEM.

There really is no excuse for a cook with at least some time on her hands to have to buy chicken or beef stock from the store. Gather together what you have, add the appropriate spices and water and simmer for a couple of hours. If you don't know what the right ingredients would be, get a recipe. Freeze some of the stock you make and keep some handy. One good suggestion is to freeze the cuttings from vegetables and leftover meat and bones until you have enough to make stock.

- **I PROMISE TO GO THROUGH MY CUPBOARDS AND REFRIGERATOR, FIND THREE INGREDIENTS AND FIND AND COOK A RECIPE THAT USES ALL THREE.**

There are several websites that let you input a few ingredients and they will pop out a recipe for you. It's rather fun and a great way to use items that might be near their expiration dates. Check out foodnetwork.com or allrecipes.com. We did a search on allrecipes.com under their "Ingredients Search" section. We wanted a dish with chicken, almonds and carrots, but without mayonnaise. It returned 23 recipes for us. Pretty cool tool. Look at what you have available and find a recipe.

allrecipes.com

- I PROMISE TO GET MYSELF A COMPLETE CHEF'S OUTFIT.

We don't know about you, but we find that we cook better when we have the right outfit. At least that's what we tell ourselves.

Bon Appetit!

**—Julia Child and thousands of
French waiters**

Check out our website ThePromisesGame.org for further ideas from us or from other people playing The Promises Game. Or add your own ideas to the community. You too can learn to be a better cook, maybe even a great chef!

PROMISE. MEAN IT. DO IT.

CHAPTER EIGHT

THE GOLDEN RULE

"Can't we talk about something besides religion for a change?"

*D*o unto others as you would have them do unto you. Virtually every major religion and culture has its own version of what is often called The Golden Rule. In Christianity that belief is stated "And as ye would that men should do to you, do ye also to them likewise." Luke 6:31 (King James Version). In Judaism it is "And what you hate, do not do to any one." Tobit 4:15. And in Hinduism it states "This is the sum of duty: do not do to others what would cause pain if done to you." Mahabharata 5:1517. Whether you call it Karma or if it's just how your parents told you to behave, The Promises Game is an excellent tool to do some *good* in the world.

Doing *good* can involve many things. You can raise money for a good cause or collect food for a food drive. You can simply perform Good Samaritan acts of kindness for strangers or for people you know. You can volunteer at your local hospital. Or you can just make sure to be there for a friend in need. One thing that we have found through playing The Promises Game is that *giving back* is important to living a full life.

The Parable of the Good Samaritan

²⁵ And behold, a certain lawyer stood up and tested Him, saying, "Teacher, what shall I do to inherit eternal life?"

²⁶ He said to him, "What is written in the law? What is your reading *of it?*"

²⁷ So he answered and said, "'You shall love the LORD your God with all your heart, with all your soul, with all your strength, and with all your mind,' and 'your neighbor as yourself.'"

²⁸ And He said to him, "You have answered rightly; do this and you will live."

²⁹ But he, wanting to justify himself, said to Jesus, "And who is my neighbor?"

[30] Then Jesus answered and said: "A certain *man* went down from Jerusalem to Jericho, and fell among thieves, who stripped him of his clothing, wounded *him,* and departed, leaving *him* half dead. [31] Now by chance a certain priest came down that road. And when he saw him, he passed by on the other side. [32] Likewise a Levite, when he arrived at the place, came and looked, and passed by on the other side. [33] But a certain Samaritan, as he journeyed, came where he was. And when he saw him, he had compassion. [34] So he went to *him* and bandaged his wounds, pouring on oil and wine; and he set him on his own animal, brought him to an inn, and took care of him. [35] On the next day, when he departed, he took out two denarii, gave *them* to the innkeeper, and said to him, 'Take care of him; and whatever more you spend, when I come again, I will repay you.' [36] So which of these three do you think was neighbor to him who fell among the thieves?"

> *If I stop to help this man, what will happen to me?" But then the Good Samaritan came by. And he reversed the question: "If I do not stop to help this man, what will happen to him?*
>
> **—Martin Luther King Jr**

[37] And he said, "He who showed mercy on him."

Then Jesus said to him, "Go and do likewise." Luke 10:25-37 (New King James Version).

MASLOW'S HIERARCHY OF NEEDS

This chapter is about more than doing *good* for others. In the middle of the last century, Abraham Maslow developed his theories on man's "Hierarchy of Needs." He noted that certain basic human needs *have* to be met before a person can move forward to address *higher* human needs. For example, a starving woman must get food to eat before she can address higher needs such as shelter, family or creativity. Following is a diagram showing Maslow's Hierarchy of Needs in a pyramid form.

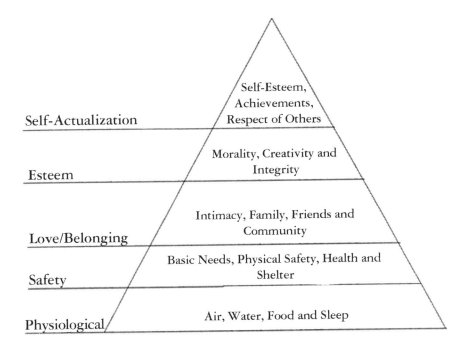

At the top of this pyramid is self-actualization. Others might call this communion with their God or Nature. Many of the previous chapter dealt with our more basic needs like cooking, home and finances. This chapter deals with Promises for man's highest needs.

> *What a man can be, he must be. This need we call self-actualization.*
>
> **—Abraham Maslow**

FIFTEEN STANDARD PROMISES

- I PROMISE TO GO TO CHURCH THIS SUNDAY.

- I PROMISE TO BAKE COOKIES FOR MY COWORKERS.

- I PROMISE TO INTRODUCE MYSELF TO THE FAMILY THAT JUST MOVED IN NEXT DOOR.

  > And while you're at it, why not bake them some cookies.

- I PROMISE TO DONATE $25 TO A CAUSE THAT I BELIEVE IN.

- I PROMISE TO HAND OUT TEN $1 BILLS TO HOMELESS PEOPLE.

- I PROMISE TO LISTEN TO INSPIRATIONAL CD'S WHILE COMMUTING TO AND FROM WORK.

- I PROMISE TO VISIT AUNT JANE IN THE HOSPICE.

- I PROMISE TO GATHER TOGETHER 15 ITEMS TO DONATE TO GOODWILL.

- I PROMISE TO VOLUNTEER AT MY LOCAL MUSEUM.

  > Or charity, soup kitchen or hospital.

- I PROMISE TO APOLOGIZE TO SUSAN FOR EMBARRASSING HER.

- I PROMISE TO COMPLIMENT MY MOTHER-IN-LAW FIVE TIMES.

- I PROMISE TO MEDITATE THREE TIMES.

For how long each time? Just make sure you are clear in your mind and in the text of your actual Promise if necessary. You could measure in minutes or emotional satisfaction or whatever you chose for your own criteria.

- I PROMISE TO PICK UP LITTER WHILE WALKING THE DOG.

- I PROMISE TO FINALLY JOIN THE CHURCH CHOIR.

- I PROMISE TO MEMORIZE A VERSE OF SCRIPTURE.

> Or memorize an inspirational poem or part of a poem. Or anything else that moves you. Being able to draw upon great inspiration, especially in times of trouble can be very comforting.

FIVE QUICK OR TIME-CREATING PROMISES

- I PROMISE TO SMILE AT THREE STRANGERS.

- I PROMISE NOT TO GOSSIP ABOUT BETTY AT WORK.

- I PROMISE TO COMPLIMENT, SINCERELY, EACH MEMBER OF MY FAMILY TWICE.

> Or maybe each of your co-workers.

- I PROMISE TO THANK THREE PEOPLE.

> You can thank your mailman, the army sergeant who lives next door, the bus driver, your teacher, your pastor, a fireman or a police officer.

- I PROMISE TO NOT YELL OUT OF ANGER.

SIX CREATIVE PROMISES

- ## I PROMISE TO PERFORM FIVE ANONYMOUS ACTS OF CHARITY.

    We have all seen the bumper sticker. It reads "Practice Random Acts Of Kindness And Senseless Acts Of Beauty." The quote has been attributed to Anne Herbert. This particular quirky creative Promise is inspired by this bumper sticker quote. The twist to this Promise that gives it its unique aspect is the word 'anonymous.' By anonymous we mean that no one, including the benefactors of your charity will know that you were the source. This is a lot harder than you think.

- ## I PROMISE TO MAKE A VALUES BOARD.

    A values board is a poster board that you create to display pictures, articles, quotes or similar items. These items are intended to represent your or your family's values. Hang it somewhere prominent to view regularly.

- ## I PROMISE TO TEACH MY CHILDREN THE PARABLE OF THE GOOD SAMARITAN AND CONDUCT A FAMILY ACTIVITY TO PUT IT INTO PRACTICE.

    The parable is found in Luke Chapter 10: 25-37. Once you have taught them this parable, come up with a way to implement its teachings in your family's life. Maybe you can collect toys for children at an orphanage. You could volunteer as a family to work at a soup kitchen for the homeless.

- I PROMISE TO FAST FOR 24 HOURS AND DONATE THE MONEY I WOULD HAVE SPENT ON FOOD TO A CHARITY TO FEED THE HOMELESS.

  Mormons have been doing this for years.

- I PROMISE TO DO FIVE NICE THINGS FOR ROGER AT WORK THIS WEEK.

  We have all encountered our 'Rogers' in this world. You know the type. He is never happy, always complaining about something or someone and in general he makes everyone else's life difficult. Lao-Tze, the great Chinese sage stated "He is kind to the kind; he is also kind to the unkind: for Virtue is kind. He is faithful to the faithful; he is also faithful to the unfaithful: for Virtue is faithful." *Tao Te Ching* Chapter 49.

- I PROMISE TO ATTEND A DIFFERENT RELIGION'S HOUSE OF WORSHIP.

  Keep an open mind. They might have something that will inspire or motivate you.

You can spend a lot of time trying to earn more money, lose weight and cook like an Iron Chef. But at some point, you will hear the clarion call to look beyond yourself and address the highest human needs; the needs at the top of Maslow's hierarchy of needs. We Promise that by devoting some of your energies to helping others, you will help yourself even more.

PROMISE. MEAN IT. DO IT.

CHAPTER NINE

"... AND THE PURSUIT OF HAPPINESS"

"You should be back at the office.
Vacations are for lazy people!
What have you accomplished today?"

In the U.S. Declaration of Independence it states that "We hold these truths to be self-evident, that all men are created equal, that they are endowed by their Creator with certain unalienable Rights, that among these are Life, Liberty and the Pursuit of Happiness." We have been spending a lot of time in this book on some serious matters. We have been focusing on health, finance, fitness, money, and homes. But The Promises Game should help you enjoy your life as well as improve your life. In fact, enjoying your life is critical to helping you accomplish the substantive achievements that you desire. Enjoying life might include having a great vacation or a long weekend. It might be as simple as finding the time to see a movie that you want to see or go fishing.

Happiness is about more than just travel and vacations. Hobbies and sports provide you with a great deal of satisfaction and relaxation. Maybe you want to take up tennis. Has quilting always fascinated you? Who says you are too old to learn a couple of chords on the guitar? Maybe there is something that you already do as a hobby or a sport, but that you would like to take to the next level of expertise.

All 50 States And A Big Ball Of Twine

"I was 13, I think, when I developed an intense desire to visit all 50 states. Living for several years on both coasts and traveling extensively for business really helped me hit most of the states. But I finally stalled out with five left to visit and it did not look like I would visit them unless I made a concerted effort to do so. Fortunately, they all touched each other such that a well-thought-out plan could accomplish my childhood dream. The summer of 2005 it was my goal to finally visit the last five states. I used The Promises Game to make it happen. It took a lot of planning and several weeks of great Promises. Although the states touched each other, they were large. Kansas, Iowa, Nebraska, South Dakota and North Dakota. I wanted to visit each state capital, spend the night in each state, and visit something famous in each one. I made Promises to plan the trip, Promises to research what was famous in each state, Promises to make reservations and Promises to find things to keep me entertained during the long drives (in this case audio college lectures on CD).

Unfortunately, none of my friends felt inclined to join me on this journey through the wheat and sunflower fields of the Plains States. I flew into Kansas City. I proceeded to mark the final five off one-by-one. Kansas, then Iowa, Nebraska and South Dakota. Finally, I arrived at my goal, North Dakota, number 50. I got off the interstate just before the border and found a country road where I could walk into my 50th state. Yeah I know, corny. It was the Midwest after all!

I did indeed touch each of the five states' capitals, spend the night in each state and visit something arguably famous in each one. In Kansas, it was the World's Largest Ball of Twine, in Cawker City." *Valfrid*

So don't forget to have some fun and enjoy life while we are here. Even if your fun is a bit nerdy, like visiting all 50 states and large balls of twine.

 ## FIFTEEN STANDARD PROMISES

- I PROMISE TO FLY A KITE IN THE PARK.

Pretty simple. Pretty easy. And very effective. You can't help but relax. Have you flown a kite since you were a child?

> *You will find the truth more quickly through delight than gravity. Let out a little more string on your kite.*
>
> **— Alan Cohen**

- I PROMISE TO SEE A THEATRE SHOW.

Live theatre is so much more rewarding than most movies released these days. But if seeing a movie would make you feel better, go ahead. Promises don't have to be difficult, painful or even a stretch. That's what this chapter is all about. Don't forget to enjoy yourself along the way. You really will accomplish more in the process.

- I PROMISE TO READ A BOOK.

We are certain that this specific Promise has increased our reading in recent years many times over. It doesn't have to be an entire book, maybe just a certain number of pages depending upon how fast you read and how much time you have in the upcoming week. Take a look at the book you are going to read. Is it small print, single-spaced, or will it read much faster. How easy is it to read? Take this all into account before you make the Promise not afterwards.

Unless there is a reason to read a specific book, it is better to Promise to read a certain number of pages of any book.

The Careless Bookworm

Once Sidney Promised to read a specific book and shortly into the book, he realized that he hated reading it. He did however keep that Promise and finished that book. And it didn't get any better. Sidney was much more careful since that time with his reading Promises.

- I PROMISE TO GO TO AN AMUSEMENT PARK WITH MY FAMILY.

- I PROMISE TO GO ON A PICNIC WITH MY BOY-FRIEND.

- I PROMISE TO HOST A GAMES NIGHT AT OUR HOUSE WITH FRIENDS.

  How long has it been since you played some of those games you loved to play as a kid - Monopoly, charades or card games like poker or hearts?

- I PROMISE TO RESEARCH HOTELS IN SAN FRAN-CISCO.

  An important part of maximizing your fun and minimizing the effects of your fun on your wallet, is proper planning. Planning and researching for the

  Travel is fatal to prejudice, bigotry and narrow-mindedness.

  — Mark Twain

future are very legitimate Promises. Just make sure that you can readily determine whether you have kept your Promise. Just thinking about your vacation to San Francisco really isn't enough to constitute keeping a Promise. Maybe you would need to make a reservation to keep this Promise. Just be clear in your mind and in your Promise what you are actually Promising.

- I PROMISE TO GO TO A KARAOKE BAR THIS WEEK AND SING.
- I PROMISE TO DRAW A SKETCH OF MY CAT.
- I PROMISE TO VISIT THE BOTANICAL GARDENS.
- I PROMISE TO PLAY TENNIS WITH JOHN THREE TIMES.
- I PROMISE TO GO ON A DOUBLE DATE WITH MY WIFE AND OUR BEST FRIENDS.
- I PROMISE TO WALK THE DOG FIVE TIMES.
- I PROMISE TO PLAY GOLF THIS WEEKEND.
- I PROMISE TO PLAY THE PIANO FOR AN HOUR.

FIVE QUICK OR TIME-CREATING PROMISES

- I PROMISE TO FAKE BEING HAPPY FOR THREE HOURS.

    Sometimes if you want to develop a certain trait or mood, first just fake it, like an actor. "Fake it 'til you make it." In this case, if you are down in the dumps all the time, set aside some time this week to fake or act being happy. In this case, maybe three straight hours, or one hour, three times over the week. Your goal is to have someone, at least think, "gosh, she's in a good mood today." It might not work for everyone, but a lot of you will actually start feeling happier to match your acting. It can't hurt. It might help. And it won't take up any time.

**"Your bad attitude was starting to affect
the others. That's much better."**

- I PROMISE TO EAT A BANANA SPLIT.

    Is there something that you love to eat but haven't
    had in a long time. Maybe you haven't had it since
    you were a kid. If it's not a banana split, maybe it's
    cotton candy, bubble gum ice cream or pop rocks.
    Treat yourself!

- I PROMISE TO JOIN A BOOK CLUB.

    If you don't have time to read this week then just
    join the group and start when time is available.

- I PROMISE TO SUBSCRIBE TO A MAGAZINE THAT
  I LIKE.

- I PROMISE TO BUY TICKETS ON-LINE FOR A COM-
  EDY SHOW.

FIVE CREATIVE PROMISES

- I PROMISE TO DANCE THIS WEEK, EVEN IF IT'S IN MY KITCHEN.

  "When I was in high school I had a girlfriend whose parents were probably twice as fun as we were at the time. They were both professors at a prestigious university and every time I saw them they were working hard on some sort of project. Except on Fridays. Every Friday they would go out dancing. One Friday they weren't able to make it out due to weather. The kitchen lights were turned to low and a mixed dance CD was put in the stereo. For the next two hours they danced in the kitchen and had a blast. Eventually we joined in. How could I ever forget that evening. Thanks Ursula and John!" *Christopher*

- I PROMISE TO PLAY HIDE AND GO SEEK WITH MY CHILDREN AND THEIR FRIENDS.

  When was the last time you played with your kids? When was the last time you played hide and go seek?

- I PROMISE TO MAKE A QUILT OUT OF PATCHES FROM MY FAMILY'S OLD CLOTHES.

- I PROMISE TO CURL UP ON THE COUCH, MAKE POPCORN AND WATCH MY FAVORITE MOVIE AGAIN.

- I PROMISE TO ENJOY THE THREE DAY WEEKEND VACATION THAT I AM TAKING.

This violates one of The Promises Game rules - that Promises have to be quantifiable and easy to determine whether or not you have kept the Promise in question. We are granting a special dispensation for this Promise. This is the exception that proves the rule. This Promise is for the workaholic that can work and plan and prepare, but never enjoy. To make this more quantifiable you could change the Promise to only checking work email once a day (or not at all if that is practical). For some people learning how to enjoy and relax is difficult, but critical. If it helps, we assure you that you will work better and more effectively after your three days relaxing.

So go ahead and pursue a little happiness while you solve all the rest of the world's problems or at least your own little corner of the world's problems.

PROMISE. MEAN IT. DO IT.

CHAPTER TEN

THE DARING, THE ODD AND THE MISFITS

© 2002 by Randy Glasbergen.
www.glasbergen.com

"What some people fail to grasp, Larry, is the difference
between 'thinking outside of the box' and just being a weirdo."

This is our last chapter on specific areas for Promises. This is the chapter for all of those misfit Promises that people have come up with over the years. They do not necessarily fit comfortably into any of the previous chapters. Often these odd Promises were also the most memorable ones.

Promise to do something that scares you just a little bit. If you are shy around strangers, you might Promise to have a three-minute conversation with three different strangers in public this week. If you have had the same hairstyle since 1999, maybe you could Promise to get a totally different hairstyle or even shave your head.

I PROMISE TO BORROW A SKATEBOARD AND SKATEBOARD TO THE OFFICE ONE DAY THIS WEEK.

This is not about skateboarding. This section of Promises is about doing something that is totally out of character for you,

> *Follow the yellow brick road.*
>
> **— The Wizard of Oz**

but that would make you feel good or otherwise expand your horizons. Whew! That is a tall order and could probably encompass an entire book. These Promises are about your comfort zone. We will just scratch the surface and set you off to explore your own bold breaks from your comfort zone. It would probably be a very stressful world if we could not rely on the certainty and safety that we experience from our unique comfort zone. However, everyone could benefit from expanding their comfort zone.

What is a stretch for one person might seem ho-hum for someone else. Examine your comfort zone and make a Promise that busts out of it on a single instance (or multiple instances) or that expands your comfort zone.

I PROMISE TO SMILE AT THREE STRANGERS EVERY DAY.

There are some people that smile at everyone all day long. You happy folk can move on to the next Promise. For many of the rest of us, the world is not

> *If you want to make people like you ... smile.*
>
> **— Dale Carnegie**

always as cheerful a place. This Promise aims at making the world around you more pleasant through the use of a friendly smile. At the same time you will make yourself happier. And yes, some people will think you are odd or nuts. In fact, if no one thinks you are odd, maybe you didn't try hard enough.

So go out and smile at three strangers each and every day and see what happens. When we mean strangers we really mean total strangers. That is people whom you do not know at all and people that you are not otherwise interacting with. That would mean that the store clerk that you are buying something from would not count. If you are a store clerk, it would not include your customers.

There are some cute variations on this Promise. You could instead Promise to get three strangers to smile at you each day. A little harder, but still manageable. Push it a little more and try to get three strangers to laugh or at least chuckle. Just go out a spread a little sunshine in the world.

I PROMISE TO CONTACT THREE FRIENDS I HAVE NOT BEEN IN TOUCH WITH FOR A WHILE.

In today's Facebook and Twitter society, it has become much easier to stay in contact with all of our friends and family. Yet still it is often not enough to just check out their Facebook page. Sometimes you need to have real-time direct contact with them. Catch up with friends that are drifting out of your life. The pace of today's society makes it easy to fall out of contact with people that we want to keep in touch with. So make it a Promise.

Maybe you want to reconnect with a specific old friend. Finding old friends has gotten a lot easier with the internet and various social networking sites. Still, it can take some effort and a little luck to find your best friend from high school 15 years later. These type of searches are best left to process-oriented Promises (that is to say you Promise to do certain steps to find this person, such as check the social networking sites and contact three mutual friends) rather than a results-oriented Promise (actually Promising to find you best friend from high school). But the choice is yours. Sometimes we need the pressure of a results-oriented Promise to accomplish some important results in our lives.

"I grew up in Montreal, Quebec, in an English-speaking suburb. Because of the rising political tensions, a lot of English Montrealers ended up leaving Quebec for other parts of Canada and the United States. As such, I lost track of most of my high school friends. Recently I felt a strong desire to find out what had happened to some of them. So, I made various steps in the process Promises. It was a lot harder than I expected because I had so little information to go on. I quickly learned that searching for Bob Smith, not knowing where he might live, was all but impossible. I was successful in finding two friends, both of whom had very unusual last names. I contacted both of them and it was great to catch up on over 30 years of our lives." *Valfrid*

I PROMISE TO WAJAMMY MY WHIGGLESTRUM BY SUNDAY

Say what! Is Dr. Seuss back? No. We mean by this any discrete project that is important to you. It's anything that you really want to do, even if someone else might find it odd or eccentric. It could be sky-diving, writing a book (or probably a chapter in a book) or marching in a parade.

> *Dream the Impossible Dream*
>
> — **Man of La Mancha**

To conclude, here is a list of further Promises that could be considered daring, odd or just misfits. Again, what is daring and odd for one person, might seem completely normal for another. In each instance of the Promises listed below, we are assuming that this is something unusual and helpful for you. Most of these Promises are self-explanatory.

- I PROMISE TO SIGN UP FOR SCUBA DIVING LESSONS.

- I PROMISE TO FILM A FUNNY VIDEOCLIP AND POST IT ON YOUTUBE.

- I PROMISE TO DYE MY HAIR PURPLE.

- I PROMISE TO HAVE BREAKFAST AT TIFFANNY'S.

- I PROMISE TO SERENADE MY GIRLFRIEND IN PUBLIC.

- I PROMISE TO TRY OUT FOR A TV GAME SHOW.

- I PROMISE TO LEARN HOW TO COUNT TO TEN IN MANDARIN.

- I PROMISE TO VOLUNTEER FOR A POLITICAL CAMPAIGN.

- I PROMISE TO PERFORM AT AN OPEN MIC NIGHT.

- I PROMISE TO TRY-OUT FOR A PLAY.

- I PROMISE TO HAVE MY FORTUNE READ.

- I PROMISE TO BE A NUDE FIGURE MODEL AT THE LOCAL ART SCHOOL.

So there you have it, some quirky, odd Promises to spice up your Promises. Don't be afraid to try some of these yourself. But more importantly, do not be afraid to come up with your very own quirky Promises. We would love to hear what you come up with. If you are having trouble coming up with an idea on any given week, just browse through the chapters in Part Two for ideas. We think you should be able to find something that will work for you that week. Above all, enjoy yourself and *actually* do what you want to do.

PROMISE. MEAN IT. DO IT.

PART THREE

FURTHER HELP PLAYING THE PROMISES GAME

CHAPTER ELEVEN

TYPES OF PROMISES

"If I stop to smell the roses, then all the other flowers will expect me to smell them too and I'm just too busy for that!"

The previous chapters looked at the content of a Promise. We divided Promises into essentially four different categories - Standard, Quick, Time-Creating and Creative. We focused on what each Promise was about.

In this chapter we will look at Promises a little differently. We will look at how a Promise interacts with time. We will also look at the different forms of Promises. The categories are not mutually exclusive. Certain Promises will fit into more than one category. We may get a little academic here, but we feel it will help you better understand the fundamental structure of various Promises. It will also help you play the game better.

CATEGORIES OF PROMISES, BY TIME

With respect to time, Promises can be categorized as time-intensive, quick or time-creating.

You Probably Won't Cure Cancer

"Easily, the most frustrating time I played The Promises Game was with a great person who was determined to solve all of the world's problems in one fell swoop. We eventually got through the second set of ten Promises and he quit, one week shy of full success. He said he didn't have enough time to keep Promises. Every week he made these incredibly aggressive and very admirable Promises. But the pressure was too great on him. I wasn't very experienced at playing The Promises Game at the time, so I wasn't much help. Now I realize that The Promises Game really isn't about 'curing cancer,' and your Promises don't need to take up a lot of time, or even any time. In fact, your Promises can *create time*." *Valfrid*

Time-Intensive Promises

Time-Intensive - that's easy. It's going to take a lot of time to keep this Promise. Don't make time-intensive Promises unless you have enough *time*! Your Promises don't have to be time-intensive, and yet many people struggle by making too many time-intensive Promises. One-third of The Promises Game is keeping your Promises. The other two-thirds is making Promises that you can keep and that will move you forward in your life. If you are short on time, don't make time-intensive Promises.

Here are three examples of time-intensive Promises:

- I PROMISE TO GO TO THE GYM SIX TIMES.

- I PROMISE TO READ A 300-PAGE BOOK.

- I PROMISE TO CLEAN OUT THE GARAGE.

Quick Promises

The next category of time-related Promises is *Quick* Promises. These are Promises that are not time-intensive, but they don't necessarily create time either. They are *quick*. They might involve actions that you have been procrastinating. These are things that you know you should do, but for whatever reason, it just doesn't happen. For example, "I Promise to make a doctor's appointment for a physical." You know you need to, but spending the 60 seconds it takes to call the doctor's office just hasn't happened.

When people first consider playing The Promises Game, they sometimes look at ten Promises in one week and get scared. The problem is that they think they have to perform ten time-intensive Promises. In fact, most of your Promises should consume no more than ten extra minutes of your time in a week. Many of the Promises you make should be quick or time-creating. That's the only way to succeed at the higher levels of Promises.

Here are three examples of quick Promises:

- I PROMISE TO CHECK MY TIRES' AIR PRESSURE.

- I PROMISE TO TELL MY WIFE I LOVE HER.

- I PROMISE TO SEND BOB AND SUSAN A THANK YOU NOTE FOR LAST WEEK'S DINNER PARTY.

Time-Creating Promises

Time-Creating - these are Promises that don't take any time at all, in fact they create time. They are often negative Promises. Do you really *not* have any time to *not* watch TV this week?

Here are three examples of time-creating Promises:

- I PROMISE TO GET UP 30 MINUTES EARLIER EACH WORKDAY.

- I PROMISE TO HIRE MY NEIGHBOR'S KID TO MOW THE LAWN.

- I PROMISE NOT TO GO OUT DRINKING AT THE BAR THIS WEEK.

CATEGORIES OF PROMISES, BY FORM

Promises can also be divided into at least nine different categories with respect to their form or structure. These are affirmative, negative, results-oriented, conditional, alternative, multiple, aggregate, component and preparatory Promises.

Affirmative Promises

The first and most common type of Promise is an *Affirmative Promise*. This is what most people think of when they think about Promises. The majority of the Promises that you make while playing The Promises Game will probably be affirmative Promises. An affirmative Promise is a commitment to do something. You could call affirmative Promises the garden-variety Promises. Affirmative Promises establish the base from which we can analyze the other types of Promises.

Here are three examples of affirmative Promises:

- I PROMISE TO GO TO THE GYM FOUR TIMES.

- I PROMISE TO ORGANIZE MY FILING CABINET.

- I PROMISE TO FLOSS MY TEETH DAILY.

Negative Promises

A *Negative Promise* is the opposite of an affirmative Promise. Instead of Promising to do something, you are Promising not to do something. Negative Promises feel almost as familiar as affirmative Promises. In a good Promises Game, you would probably want to use a smattering of negative Promises to augment your affirmative Promises. Negative Promises are also often quick or time-creating Promises.

Here are three examples of negative Promises:

- I PROMISE NOT TO WATCH TELEVISION THIS WEEK.

- I PROMISE NOT TO EAT AT A FAST FOOD RESTAURANT.

- I PROMISE NOT TO YELL AT MY KIDS.

Results-Oriented Promises

A *Results-Oriented Promise* is the granddaddy of all Promises. It is possible to Promise to get the results, rather than just Promise to perform the process. Almost all of the other types of Promises concentrate on what you are going to do (or not do) with the expectation that if you accomplish these steps, they will cause a result that you desire. Results-oriented Promises focus only on the results, not the steps in the process.

Here are three examples of results-oriented Promises:

- I PROMISE TO GET A JOB OFFER FROM THE ACME COMPANY.

A Job Offer

> Kitty made the bold Promise that she would get a new job offer that very week. She had been at her job for ten years and had started a job search a few weeks earlier with little success. Kitty made the Promise, got an offer for more than she was making at her then-current job and she accepted the offer. Now that's a results-oriented Promise!

- I PROMISE TO GET AN A ON MY MID-TERM.

- I PROMISE TO EARN $2,000 IN COMMISSIONS THIS WEEK.

Conditional Promises

A *Conditional Promise* is a Promise to do something if something else happens. There should be significant probability on your part that the condition precedent (that is the event that must precede the need for fulfilling your Promise) will occur.

Here are three examples of conditional Promises:

- I PROMISE TO GET MY DAUGHTER A NEW BIKE IF SHE GETS AN A ON HER MATH TEST.

- I PROMISE TO RIDE MY BIKE TO WORK EVERYDAY THIS WEEK UNLESS IT RAINS.

- I PROMISE TO REPAY MY BROTHER THE $100 I BORROWED FROM HIM, IF I SELL MY TV ON CRAIGSLIST.

If the condition precedent does not occur, you don't have to carry out the rest of the Promise. For example, if your daughter does not get an A on her math test, you don't have to get her a new bike. The Promise would be considered kept.

116

Alternative Promises

Sometimes you are not sure what is going to happen next week. There may be two possibilities. An *Alternative Promise* is a Promise where you Promise to do one of two things. Completing either one of the two would keep your Promise. The two alternatives should have some rational connection.

Here are three examples of alternative Promises:

- I PROMISE TO MAKE DINNER FOR MY WIFE ON FRIDAY OR TAKE HER TO HER FAVORITE RESTAURANT. I PROMISE TO TAKE MY FAMILY TO EITHER DISNEYLAND OR SIX FLAGS.

- I PROMISE TO PLAY TENNIS WITH BOB OR PLAY GOLF WITH JIM.

Combination Promises

Whereas an alternative Promise was an "A or B" Promise, a *Combination Promise* is an "A and B" Promise. You are Promising to do two related actions. It's important that they be somehow related. With a combination Promise, make sure that both parts are important. Don't Promise to do A and B, if only A is important to you. In that case, just make Promise A.

Here are three examples of combination Promises:

- I PROMISE TO CLEAN OUT THE GARAGE AND THE HALL CLOSET.

- I PROMISE TO SIGN UP FOR A COOKING CLASS AND GET A NEW SET OF KNIVES.

- I PROMISE TO TAKE MY SON TO THE ZOO AND TAKE MY DAUGHTER TO A CUBS GAME.

Aggregate Promises

An *Aggregate Promise* is a Promise where you will do a total amount of something, but you don't detail when or how often you will work on it. For example, I Promise to jog a total of ten miles this week, is an aggregate Promise. You are not Promising to jog ten miles in a single day or two miles a day for five days or any other combination. You are just Promising to reach ten miles, in the aggregate, by the end of the week.

Here are three more examples of aggregate Promises:

- I PROMISE TO SPEND A TOTAL OF FIVE HOURS PRACTICING THE PIANO.

- I PROMISE TO COLD CALL 20 POTENTIAL CLIENTS.

- I PROMISE TO WRITE TEN PAGES IN MY BOOK.

Component Promises

A *Component Promise* is a Promise that would normally take longer than a week to accomplish. The Promises Game is based upon Promises that can be completed in one week. The classic example would be reading a book. If you want to read a book that is 250 pages long, but based upon your reading speed and the amount of time you expect to have available, you can only reasonably expect to read half the book. You could divide reading the entire book down into its component parts. In this case, you Promise to read the first half this week, with the expectation, but not the Promise, that you will read the last half next week. A component Promise is the solution.

Here are three more examples of component Promises:

- I PROMISE TO SEND OUT THANK YOU CARDS TO ONE-HALF OF THE PEOPLE THAT SENT US WEDDING GIFTS.

- I PROMISE TO REOGANIZE THE FOUR UPPER DRAWERS IN MY DRESSER.

- I PROMISE TO COMPLETE ONE-HALF OF MY EMPLOYEE REVIEWS.

Preparatory Promises

The final type of Promise is a *Preparatory Promise*. Preparatory Promises are often planning Promises. Sometimes a large project needs some planning first. If you decide that you need to lose ten pounds, but have no idea how to do it, a preparatory Promise will help you. For example, if you want to lose ten pounds in the next four months, but have no idea how to do it, a good preparatory Promise would be to research and select a diet and exercise program. This is a preparatory Promise. Presumably in the subsequent weeks you will implement the plan that you selected this week.

Here are three examples of preparatory Promises:

- I PROMISE TO GO TO A COUNSELOR AT SCHOOL TO DECIDE WHAT CLASSES I NEED TO TAKE TO GRADUATE ON TIME.

- I PROMISE TO GET A BOOK ON HOW TO BREW BEER.

- I PROMISE TO OUTLINE MY TERM PAPER.

PROMISE. MEAN IT. DO IT.

CHAPTER TWELVE

HELPFUL HINTS

© Randy Glasbergen.
www.glasbergen.com

"This matter requires immediate action.
I'll get someone to ignore it right away!"

This chapter is a collection of ideas and lessons that we have learned about The Promises Game that we hope will help you be more successful when you play. We also hope that these helpful hints will motivate you when you have challenges playing the game and clarify any questions you may have. We have played The Promises Game for over eight years now and we have learned a thing or two along the way. We also are sure that we will learn a whole lot more from your experiences.

Helpful Hint #1: Harness the Power of Panic. Front-Load, Front-Load, Front-Load!

Sometimes when you have an important project that has a firm deadline, you leave most of the work until the very end. You procrastinated or were just very busy. If the deadline is inflexible, you have to pack a lot of work into the last few hours. Adrenaline, even panic, kicks in and you find that you finish the project on time. This will happen to you when you play The Promises Game.

At some point you will have four Promises that need to be completed and about four hours left in the week to do them. It should take you twice the time, but somehow, some way you will find the energy, ingenuity and drive to finish them.

What if you could harness just one-quarter of that adrenaline-induced power of panic and deploy it into the first four hours after making your Promises, rather than the last four hours of the week? Learn how to harness the power of panic. Immediately after you make your Promises, if appropriate, start on one or more of your Promises. Harness at least 25% of the power of panic that you usually reserve for the last four hours before a deadline. You can knock off portions of several Promises or perhaps complete one Promise in full. If you have Promised to jog for two hours in the aggregate this week, why not jog for 20 minutes right away? If you Promised to set up a dentist appointment, why not pick up the phone as you are leaving your Promises Meeting and set it up immediately? If you Promise to clean out the hall closet, why not tackle the first 15 items now?

From time immemorial, lightening was something to be feared. It caused dread, fire and death. But lightening is just electricity in the sky. One day, man learned to harness that deadly energy and created the modern, illuminated world that we live in today. Panic is like lightening. Learn to harness it.

This is called 'front-loading.' We think that after learning how to keep your Promises and how to make good Promises, this is the third most important thing that you can learn from playing The Promises Game. Not only will you find that your Promises will be easier to keep, but by taking some initial action, you might find yourself taking even more action right away. If you Promise to weed all of your flower beds and then immediately decide to start on one

The best way to get something done is to begin.

—Unknown

flower bed, before you even know it, you could easily have finished the entire project. You will feel great about yourself and your completing the remainder of your Promises will be just that much easier. Harness just a little panic in the first four hours rather than the last four hours and you will amaze yourself with how much you can accomplish.

Helpful Hint #2: Keep A Written Record Of Your Promises And Your Performance.

One of our biggest regrets is that we didn't keep detailed written records of all of the Promises that we made and our successes and failures with

I write down everything I want to remember. That way, instead of spending a lot of time trying to remember what it is I wrote down, I spend the time looking for the paper I wrote it down on.

—Beryl Pfizer

them. What Promises do you keep making over and over again? Which Promises do you fail to keep? Are you really pushing yourself hard enough? Could you have made better Promises? Which Promises were just too easy? By reviewing these records, you will be able to make better Promises in the future and accomplish more playing the game. This is why we developed the Weekly Promises Logs in the Appendix. Use these logs to record each of your weekly Promises, as well as your Promises Partner's Promises. Retain all of them for future reference.

Helpful Hint #3: Keep A Copy Of Your Current Promises And Place It Somewhere Visible To You.

In a busy week it is easy to forget what Promises you have made. It's "out of sight, out of mind." Put you Weekly Promises Log or at least a list of your Promises in a prominent place (or even in more than one place) where you will see your Promises regularly. You could place it on the bathroom mirror, your refrigerator or next to your computer screen. Just make sure that you see your Promises regularly so that you won't forget one of your Promises. You can also check them off as you keep your Promises in whole or in part.

Helpful Hint # 4: If You Fail To Keep One Promise, Keep The Rest Of Your Promises.

What happens if you make a Promise that you fail to keep, especially if you fail to keep it early in the week? Let's say that you Promise not to smoke any cigarettes this week and on the second day you smoke three cigarettes. The Promise cannot be kept and therefore you and your

> *It was character that got us out of bed, commitment that moved us into action, and discipline that enabled us to follow through.*
>
> **—Zig Ziglar**

Promises Partner will not keep all of your Promises this week. Here is where your character will be revealed. Firstly, you should not inform your Promises Partner that you have already failed. That may discourage him from finishing his own Promises and gaining the benefits he would receive from keeping his Promises. Secondly, and most importantly, you should strive to keep all of the rest of your Promises as if you had not failed on a Promise. This can be very hard to do. The temptation is to "take a break" this week and just let everything slide. Show the resolve to still keep the rest of your Promises.

Helpful Hint #5: During The Week, Keep A List Of Potential Future Promises.

Throughout the week ideas will come up for potential future Promises. Write them down in one place and keep them handy. Even deciding to repeat a former Promise could go on this list. When it comes time to decide upon you next Promises, review this list. Don't wait until the last minute to decide on your next Promises. That is a recipe for disaster. Use the Weekly Promises Log to write down ideas for future Promises when you think of them. Go back to this list when you are ready to make your next week's Promises.

Helpful Hint #6: Is A Perfect Game Our Goal?

A perfect game can be accomplished in ten weeks. To the best of our knowledge, it has only happened once. On one hand, it is important to keep all of your Promises, therefore your goal should be perfection. At the same time, the true importance of The Promises Game is each player's growth and

> *Perfection is not obtainable, but if we chase perfection we can catch excellence.*
>
> **—Vince Lombardi**

accomplishments. But in the end we have to say yes, your goal has to be a perfect game. But don't beat yourself up for failures. You've got plenty of company. The very first two people to play The Promises Game, Kitty and Valfrid, took over one year to finish. Most games last about 13-16 weeks.

Helpful Hint #7: You Can Skip A Week If Either Of You Cannot Control Your Time

We have discussed that it's fine to skip a week when making Promises just isn't the right course of action for that week. The classic example is when you or your Promises Partner goes on a vacation. The rationale here is that you might not want to pre-structure your vacation time, especially if there are more people involved than just yourself. What if you were planning to take your family to Paris for a vacation and decide to Promise to spend two days at The Louvre? That would be a great Promise. But not if after the first three hours at the museum every other member of your family was bored and wanted to do something else. With vacations, especially involving other people, you may need to retain more flexibility than The Promises Game can offer you. Skip a week.

However, if you are the type of person who always ends up with poorly planned, meandering vacations that you end up wishing you had organized better, then maybe making Promises during a vacation is the perfect solution to your problems. Promise to at least visit the Louvre (maybe not for two days). Promise to take a family picture at the Eiffel Tower. Promise to order at least one meal using the high school French that you brushed up on before leaving for France.

Difficult work situations are other times when you might need to be consider skipping a week. Sometimes projects or business trips can be so uncertain in advance that you cannot make meaningful Promises. A trip to Florida to negotiate a contract could take a day or stretch out for five days. A sales trip under the control of your unpredictable boss can present untold complications to Promises. Special events, like company retreats or family reunions, can also make Promises difficult to come up with and even more difficult to keep.

Health problems are another area of concern. If you or a loved one, especially one of your children is sick or injured, you may not be in control of enough of your time to make and keep Promises. Your health and your family's health come first. The more uncertain you are of the seriousness of the illness or injury involved, the more cautious you should be about making Promises for the upcoming week. And maybe you should just skip a week.

Helpful Hint #8: Your Promises Partner Is Not Working Out

This is a difficult problem. Some people do not take The Promises Game seriously. Others take it too seriously. The Promises Game is just a tool and it isn't right for everyone. Problems can arise. Partners can miss meetings or not return phone calls. Others may just not take it seriously and never keep their Promises. You have to decide when to call it quits if it's not working for you. You want a Promise Partner who will challenge you with their enthusiasm or ability and you should do the same for them. Sometimes people just need a little push but other times they are just not ready pursue their goals. If it's not working for the two of you, call it quits and start over with someone new. Don't make a big deal of it. It's just a game.

He's just not that into you.

**— Greg Behrendt &
Liz Tuccillo**

Helpful Hint #9: Play it Again!

Some people are satisfied playing The Promises Game just once. We both have played over and over again. Every game is wonderfully unique. We learn something new each time. Each game has offered different dynamics and created more results than before.

> *Play it again, Sam.*
>
> **—Casablanca
> (not actually!)**

The Promises Game has many levels. Initially, playing the game is about learning how to keep your Promises. The next level is learning how to make Promises that you are able to keep. The third level that we have discovered is to use the game to push your boundaries and accomplish things you never expected possible.

A couple of thoughts about playing multiple games. First, don't start a new game with the same Promises Partner. It detracts from the completeness of the first game. Pick someone new for a different experience. It's acceptable to play later games with former Promises Partners, just not back-to-back. Some people like to take a short break in between games, a week or two. Our thought is that after you have just finished three straight weeks of ten Promises, starting anew at the three Promises level will feel like a vacation. Each new game is a new opportunity to learn something about yourself and accomplish more in your life. Take advantage of it.

Helpful Hint #10: Your Next Promises Partner

If you decide to play The Promises Game again, you will need to find a new Promises Partner. It is not a good idea to play the game back-to-back with the same Promises Partner. The best person to select your next Promises Partner is your former Promises Partner. The first time each of us played The Promises Game, our Promises Partner selected out our next Promises Partner. It worked well for us.

Once you have played the game with a new Promises Partner, it's ok to go back to a former Promises Partner. It can be fun to play with a previous Promises Partner and share what you have learned and try out new Promises and ideas from other Promises Partners and games.

> *Variety's the very spice of life That gives it all its flavour.*
>
> **—William Cowper**

HARNESS THE POWER OF PANIC. FRONT-LOAD, FRONT-LOAD, FRONT- LOAD!

And really our most important helpful hint is our first one. Harness the power of panic. Front-load, front-load, front-load! If you could put even 25% of the panic that you experience when something *has* to be completed in the next four hours, into the first four hours of that project, your life would be changed beyond belief, and you will *actually* do what you want to do! Front-load, Front-load, Front-load!

HELPFUL HINTS
IN A NUTSHELL

1. Harness the power of panic. Front-load, front-load, front-load!

2. Keep a written record of all of your Promises and success or failure at keeping those Promises. Use the Weekly Promises Log.

3. Keep a copy of your current Promises in a place regularly visible to you.

4. If you fail to keep one Promise, work on the remaining Promises just as hard as you otherwise would have.

5. Keep a written list of potential future Promises.

6. Aim for a perfect game, but don't be overwhelmed by some failure.

7. If you or your Promises Partner do not believe you can control enough of your time in the next week to keep all of your Promises, you probably should skip that week and start up again later.

8. If you and your Promises Partner aren't working out together, cut your losses and select a new Partner.

9. Play The Promises Game again and again. It's a tool that you can use for the rest of your life.

10. Have your former Promises Partner select your next Promises Partner.

PROMISE. MEAN IT. DO IT.

APPENDIX

THE PROMISES GAME

WEEKLY PROMISES LOGS

MY NAME:

MY PROMISE PARTNER'S NAME:

NUMBER OF PROMISES:

DATE:

DATE, TIME & PLACE OF NEXT PROMISES MEETING:

MY PROMISES   MY PROMISES PARTNER'S

1.	1.
2.	2.
3.	3.
4.	4.
5.	5.
6.	6.
7.	7.
8.	8.
9.	9.
10.	10.

NOTES

POSSIBLE PROMISES FOR NEXT WEEK

Regularly keeping your Promises, otherwise called reliability or dependability, is a character trait. Like most character traits, it must be acquired and nurtured.

PROMISE. MEAN IT. DO IT.

MY NAME:

MY PROMISE PARTNER'S NAME:

NUMBER OF PROMISES:

DATE:

DATE, TIME & PLACE OF NEXT PROMISES MEETING:

MY PROMISES   MY PROMISES PARTNER'S

MY PROMISES	MY PROMISES PARTNER'S
1.	1.
2.	2.
3.	3.
4.	4.
5.	5.
6.	6.
7.	7.
8.	8.
9.	9.
10.	10.

NOTES

POSSIBLE PROMISES FOR NEXT WEEK

Panic is like lighting. Learn to harness it.
Front-Load, Front-Load, Front-Load!

PROMISE. MEAN IT. DO IT.

MY NAME:

MY PROMISE PARTNER'S NAME:

NUMBER OF PROMISES:

DATE:

DATE, TIME & PLACE OF NEXT PROMISES MEETING:

MY PROMISES   MY PROMISES PARTNER'S

MY PROMISES	MY PROMISES PARTNER'S
1.	1.
2.	2.
3.	3.
4.	4.
5.	5.
6.	6.
7.	7.
8.	8.
9.	9.
10.	10.

NOTES

POSSIBLE PROMISES FOR NEXT WEEK

Are you the type of person who Promises to be somewhere at 6:00 and no one expects you until 7:00? Or are you the type of person who Promises to be somewhere at 6:00 and if you haven't arrived by 6:05 people worry that you had an accident?

PROMISE. MEAN IT. DO IT.

MY NAME:

MY PROMISE PARTNER'S NAME:

NUMBER OF PROMISES:

DATE:

DATE, TIME & PLACE OF NEXT PROMISES MEETING:

MY PROMISES   MY PROMISES PARTNER'S

1.	1.
2.	2.
3.	3.
4.	4.
5.	5.
6.	6.
7.	7.
8.	8.
9.	9.
10.	10.

NOTES

POSSIBLE PROMISES FOR NEXT WEEK

If you never gain ten extra pounds,
it's impossible to gain 50 extra pounds.

PROMISE. MEAN IT. DO IT.

MY NAME:
MY PROMISE PARTNER'S NAME:
NUMBER OF PROMISES:
DATE:
DATE, TIME & PLACE OF NEXT PROMISES MEETING:

MY PROMISES	MY PROMISES PARTNER'S
1.	1.
2.	2.
3.	3.
4.	4.
5.	5.
6.	6.
7.	7.
8.	8.
9.	9.
10.	10.

NOTES

POSSIBLE PROMISES FOR NEXT WEEK

Post your Promises.
Keep a list of your Promises somewhere where you will see it often.

PROMISE. MEAN IT. DO IT.

MY NAME:

MY PROMISE PARTNER'S NAME:

NUMBER OF PROMISES:

DATE:

DATE, TIME & PLACE OF NEXT PROMISES MEETING:

MY PROMISES   MY PROMISES PARTNER'S

1.	1.
2.	2.
3.	3.
4.	4.
5.	5.
6.	6.
7.	7.
8.	8.
9.	9.
10.	10.

NOTES

POSSIBLE PROMISES FOR NEXT WEEK

It's OK to repeat the same Promise over again.

PROMISE. MEAN IT. DO IT.

MY NAME:

MY PROMISE PARTNER'S NAME:

NUMBER OF PROMISES:

DATE:

DATE, TIME & PLACE OF NEXT PROMISES MEETING:

MY PROMISES	MY PROMISES PARTNER'S
1.	1.
2.	2.
3.	3.
4.	4.
5.	5.
6.	6.
7.	7.
8.	8.
9.	9.
10.	10.

NOTES

POSSIBLE PROMISES FOR NEXT WEEK

The Promises Game Diet- Eat Less and Exercise More.

PROMISE. MEAN IT. DO IT.

MY NAME:

MY PROMISE PARTNER'S NAME:

NUMBER OF PROMISES:

DATE:

DATE, TIME & PLACE OF NEXT PROMISES MEETING:

MY PROMISES   MY PROMISES PARTNER'S

1.	1.
2.	2.
3.	3.
4.	4.
5.	5.
6.	6.
7.	7.
8.	8.
9.	9.
10.	10.

NOTES

POSSIBLE PROMISES FOR NEXT WEEK

The only way to lose the Promises Game is to quit.

PROMISE. MEAN IT. DO IT.

MY NAME:

MY PROMISE PARTNER'S NAME:

NUMBER OF PROMISES:

DATE:

DATE, TIME & PLACE OF NEXT PROMISES MEETING:

MY PROMISES   MY PROMISES PARTNER'S

1.	1.
2.	2.
3.	3.
4.	4.
5.	5.
6.	6.
7.	7.
8.	8.
9.	9.
10.	10.

NOTES

POSSIBLE PROMISES FOR NEXT WEEK

All 50 states and a big ball of twine.

PROMISE. MEAN IT. DO IT.

MY NAME:

MY PROMISE PARTNER'S NAME:

NUMBER OF PROMISES:

DATE:

DATE, TIME & PLACE OF NEXT PROMISES MEETING:

MY PROMISES	MY PROMISES PARTNER'S
1.	1.
2.	2.
3.	3.
4.	4.
5.	5.
6.	6.
7.	7.
8.	8.
9.	9.
10.	10.

NOTES

POSSIBLE PROMISES FOR NEXT WEEK

Most of your Promises should consume no more
than ten minutes of your time in a week.

PROMISE. MEAN IT. DO IT.

Made in the USA
Lexington, KY
21 February 2013